Accession no.
36092671

D1491668

The Business of Brands

The Business of Brands

by Jon Miller & David Muir

LIS - LIBRARY

Date	Fund
13/7/09	658.827 PG MIL

Order No.
02049545

University of Chester

3 6092671

John Wiley & Sons, Ltd

Copyright © 2004   John Wiley & Sons Ltd, The Atrium, Southern Gate, Chichester,
West Sussex PO19 8SQ, England

Telephone (+44) 1243 779777

Email (for orders and customer service enquiries): cs-books@wiley.co.uk
Visit our Home Page on www.wileyeurope.com or www.wiley.com

Reprinted November 2004, June 2005

All Rights Reserved. No part of this publication may be reproduced, stored in a retrieval system or
transmitted in any form or by any means, electronic, mechanical, photocopying, recording, scan-
ning or otherwise, except under the terms of the Copyright, Designs and Patents Act 1988 or
under the terms of a licence issued by the Copyright Licensing Agency Ltd, 90 Tottenham Court
Road, London W1T 4LP, UK, without the permission in writing of the Publisher. Requests to the
Publisher should be addressed to the Permissions Department, John Wiley & Sons Ltd, The
Atrium, Southern Gate, Chichester, West Sussex PO19 8SQ, England, or emailed to
permreq@wiley.co.uk, or faxed to (+44) 1243 770620.

Designations used by companies to distinguish their products are often claimed as trademarks. All
brand names and product names used in this book are trade names, service marks, trademarks or
registered trademarks of their respective owners. The Publisher is not associated with any product
or vendor mentioned in this book.

This publication is designed to provide accurate and authoritative information in regard to the
subject matter covered. It is sold on the understanding that the Publisher is not engaged in ren-
dering professional services. If professional advice or other expert assistance is required, the services of a competent professional should be sought.

Other Wiley Editorial Offices

John Wiley & Sons Inc., 111 River Street, Hoboken, NJ 07030, USA

Jossey-Bass, 989 Market Street, San Francisco, CA 94103-1741, USA

Wiley-VCH Verlag GmbH, Boschstr. 12, D-69469 Weinheim, Germany

John Wiley & Sons Australia Ltd, 33 Park Road, Milton, Queensland 4064, Australia

John Wiley & Sons (Asia) Pte Ltd, 2 Clementi Loop #02-01, Jin Xing Distripark, Singapore
129809

John Wiley & Sons Canada Ltd, 22 Worcester Road, Etobicoke, Ontario, Canada M9W 1L1

Wiley also publishes its books in a variety of electronic formats. Some content that appears in
print may not be available in electronic books.

Library of Congress Cataloging-in-Publication Data

Miller, Jon, 1971–
The business of brands / by Jon Miller & David Muir.
p. cm.
Includes bibliographical references and index.
ISBN 0-470-86259-9 (hbk. : alk. paper)
1. Brand name products.   2. Brand name products–Marketing.   3. Brand name produts–Management.   4. Value added.   I. Muir, David. 1971-II. Title.

HD69.B7M55 2004
658.8'27–dc22   2004053025

British Library Cataloguing in Publication Data

A catalogue record for this book is available from the British Library

ISBN 10: 0-470-86259-9 (H/B)
ISBN 13: 978-0-470-86259-9 (H/B)

Typeset in Goudy and Gill sans
Printed and bound in Great Britain by Antony Rowe Ltd, Chippenham, Wiltshire
This book is printed on acid-free paper responsibly manufactured from sustainable forestry in
which at least two trees are planted for each one used for paper production.

Contents

Acknowledgements

This book is a survey of the best and the brightest thinking on brands from around the world. It's been shaped over the course of the past year by conversations with many people – idle chats, chance remarks, heated discussions and impassioned rants. In particular, we'd like to thank the following people for sharing their thoughts on branding – and agreeing to be quoted: Esther Dyson, Michel van Eesbeeck, Andy Farr, Sir Niall FitzGerald, Irwin Gotlieb, Garth Hallberg, Marie-Louise Neill, Rosemary Ryan, Steve Hayden, Jon Steel, Rory Sutherland, and Tony Wright.

We also owe special thanks to a number of people who shared their insights with us, in particular Eleanor Cooksey and Will Galgey from the Henley Centre, David Magliano, Jacqui Kean from *The Economist*, and some of our colleagues from Ogilvy, especially Andrew Daykin, Jane Hodson, Dimitri Maex and Lee Taylor.

Some people went well beyond the call of duty, volunteering to read various early manuscripts and providing invaluable feedback: special gratitude to Ashton Bishop, Tom Campbell, Vicky Moffatt and Jon Sharpe. A huge thanks to Claire Plimmer and Jo Golesworthy at John Wiley & Sons for their patience and guidance as this project slowly evolved from its early chaos into a semblance of order.

Anja Hoehne was tireless in chasing the endless copyrights paperwork – without them this book would have no pictures! Ian Patrick deserves special thanks for the great cover design. Thanks to the inimitable Charlie Wells and his forensic research skills – without which Part IV of this book wouldn't exist. We owe special gratitude to Ogilvy, and especially Mike Walsh, for sponsoring this project.

Throughout the writing of this book, Jeremy Bullmore has been a great source of ideas and encouragement, and Mark Earls has offered many useful interventions – without their help this book would be much the poorer.

Individually, David would like to thank Jon for the energy and drive on the writing of the book. Without him it wouldn't have happened. David also owes an enormous debt to Simeon Duckworth who inspired and developed much of the work seen in later parts of the book. Finally, David would like to thank Rachael for her patience and understanding as this book frequently interfered with weekends and evenings.

Jon would like to thank his parents, Caroline and Anthony, for their unfailingly optimistic approach to pretty much everything.

Needless to say, any errors, fuzzy thinking or gross stupidity is entirely our own work.

Why this Book was Written

Type the word 'brand' into Amazon and you'll get a list of 56 636 books. Why did we think that the world needed another one?

In December 2001, a new client asked us a potent question. Their dominant market position was being eroded by aggressive competitors – some large-scale activity was obviously required. So, they prepared to make a substantial investment in a campaign to revitalize their brand. What, they asked, are the broadest benefits that a strong brand can bring to a business?

As we set about answering this question, we found many pieces of the jigsaw, but no overall picture of how a strong brand can create value across a business. There was plenty of interesting material: academic studies, stories from clients, case studies, agency research, but it was scattered across journals, anecdotes, presentations and articles. As there was no single book that assembled all the learning about the business value of brands into one comprehensive survey, we decided to write one, and set out to incorporate the many stories and studies, together with some fresh research, into one thorough source book.

We didn't want to write a marketing book about branding, but a business book about the value of brands. That's why we've called it *The Business of Brands*. We've outlined many of the roles that brands can play across the complete spectrum of business activities, from human resources to product development and, of course, market share and customer value.

Brands are moving up the corporate agenda. A strong brand can create value across the business, and that's why brand investment is increasingly a strategic priority for many companies. This is a book that will provide insight and understanding for those seeking to explore the potential of their brands.

The Six-Minute Read

This section contains a quick, pre-digested, highly compressed version of *The Business of Brands*.

PART I: BRANDS AND BUSINESS

The word 'brand' has become one of the most heavily used in the business lexicon. Given that brands are the subject of this book, we begin by outlining exactly what we mean by the word. We take as our starting point the definition of brands given by David Ogilvy, who described a brand as 'the intangible sum of a product's attributes: its name, packaging, and price, its history, its reputation, and the way it is advertised'.

Of course, it's possible to agonize over a precise definition of a brand. Instead, we have identified five themes which are essential to understanding brands:

1. A brand enhances the value of a product or service beyond its functional purpose – thereby supporting volume and price.
2. A brand is a link between an organization and its stakeholders, providing a badge of continuity and trust.
3. A brand is the result of behaviour – everything an organization does has the potential to impact the brand.
4. A brand exists only in people's minds – it is a collection of feelings and perceptions in the mind of the consumer.

5. *A brand can provide an organization with purpose and direction – providing a source of motivation and interest for stakeholders.*

We believe that brands are critical to creating value within an organization. To a large extent, brand strategy is business strategy. However, some persistent misconceptions lead to a limited view of brand strategy:

- *Brand strategy is more than marketing*
  Marketing, in the strict sense, is about taking products and services to market. We believe that brands can play a wider role than growing and retaining market share.

- *Brand strategy is more than communications*
  To build a strong brand takes more than communications: it's more than what you *say* (and how you say it) – brands grow out of what you *do* (and how you do it).

- *Brand strategy is more than effectiveness*
  Effectiveness – doing something *well* – is not itself a strategy. Brands may perform well in the short term at the expense of their long-term competitive position.

- *Brand strategy is more than positioning*
  Positioning is about clearly differentiating the brand from its competitors: find a gap, and then fill it. However, positioning-led strategies often overlook the importance of awareness and of establishing points of parity.

Brand strategy, we suggest, should ultimately be regarded as an approach to building shareholder value. The most important driver of shareholder value is cash flow – we argue that a strong brand may have a positive impact on a company's cash flows. Unless we get beter at articulating the case for brands in terms of business strategy, their potential may remain unexploited.

PART II: SOURCES OF BUSINESS VALUE

Brands can create value for a business in a variety of ways – from growing and retaining market share, to attracting and retaining talented employees. We examine some potential sources of business value that strong brands can provide.

- *Strong brands command market share*
  Research shows that brand strength is correlated to market share – and also that market share is strongly linked to profitability. Further, brands enable market share to become self-reinforcing.

- *Strong brands create barriers to entry for competitors*
  Brands can play a defensive role: the costs associated with establishing a strong brand in a given category can often deter potential competitors from entering the market.

- *Strong brands can extend into new areas*
  Brands provide businesses with options for growth through brand extensions. These can allow access to new revenue streams, or help a business to respond to market changes.

- *Strong brands can enter new markets*
  Overseas markets may be a significant source of potential revenue for strong brands – provided a balance is struck between global consistency and local sensitivity.

- *Strong brands have lower price elasticity*
  Brands can support the price that a purchaser is willing to pay – a strong brand may increase prices without losing significant volume.

- *Strong brands can command a premium*
  Brands can enable businesses to charge a premium; sometimes, consumers *want* to pay more – a higher price creates a reassuring sense of superior quality.

- *Strong brands can deal with market disruption*
  Brands can help businesses to maintain performance during times of uncertainty – provided that they are flexible and open-minded in their approach to the future.

- *Strong brands can attract and retain talent*
  Brands create competitive advantage by attracting talented employees – and keeping them. This can also reduce the significant costs associated with recruiting – and re-recruiting.

- *Strong brands are a store of trust*
  Brands can engender trust among stakeholders – ultimately this is the source of real business value for an organization. Real trust comes from having a clear brand strategy and delivering upon it consistently over time.

- *Strong brands can stimulate innovation*
  Brands can help to create new ideas for products and services, providing an in-built maket-orientation to a company's research and development activities.

Each of these potential sources of business value is discussed in more detail, with case studies and further references.

PART III: STRATEGIC BRAND PLANNING

If brands strategy is business strategy, then brand planning becomes a key business imperative. We examine the principle issues in brand planning, and outline how they contribute to business success.

Defining the market

The task of defining the market is at the core of the business: a bold, insightful definition can make a powerful difference to a brand's performance. We review the issues and approaches for finding the best definition, and note that, broadly, a brand may face one of the following strategic challenges:

- *Launch* – introducing a brand to a market for the first time. (See p. 107.)
- *Challenge* – displacing dominant brands in the market, which often requires particularly ingenious planning. (See p. 116.)
- *Maintain* – defending a market position against challenges, market changes and the whims of consumers. (See p. 125.)

- *Revitalize* – bringing fresh life to an existing brand that has lost its shine. (See p. 134.)
- *Re-brand* – change the branding for a product, service or company. (See p. 141.)
- *Acquisition* – integrate an acquired brand into an existing portfolio. (See p. 151.)

All brands will encounter one or more of these issues at some point – and sometimes several at once.

PART IV: BRAND BIOGRAPHIES

In this section we pull our themes together by looking at the 'biographies' of seven well-known brands.

- *American Express:* The brand's premium status is at the heart of the company's business model.
- *Ben & Jerry's:* Employees, customers and suppliers all respond to the company's values.
- *Def Jam:* This brand has weathered the storms hitting the music industry – and even expanded into new areas.
- *IBM:* Revitalizing the brand was crucial to driving the company's famous turnaround.
- *Dove:* The strength of the brand has fuelled phenomenal growth into new countries and product areas.
- *BP:* The BP brand is a unifying force across the company's huge, diverse global operations.
- *The Economist:* Investing in the brand – as opposed to merely advertising next week's content – has yielded impressive results.

Each of these is discussed in detail, and the contribution of the brand is clearly outlined. We begin by describing the heritage of the brand, before looking at its role within the company's overall business model. Finally, an overview of the company's financial performance is given.

PART V: MEASUREMENT AND VALUATION

Understanding brand strength

Everybody recognizes that some brands are stronger than others – but what makes one brand strong, and another weak? We examine some approaches to understanding *brand equity*.

Understanding brand value

Everyone agrees that brands are valuable – but why, exactly? What makes one brand more valuable than another? We look at several approaches for valuing a brand.

The business impact of brands

Brands are clearly high on the agenda of the world's most successful companies – but why? We conducted an in-depth study which correlates brand strength with key business metrics – including shareholder value. Other key business impacts include:

- *Strong brands reduce business risk* – Clear evidence exists that strong brands are associated with lower levels of business risk.
- *Strong brands create options* – Brands can create value by opening up new areas of potential business activity.

Building strong brands

Our investigations revealed some clear characteristics that are shared by all strong brands. These provide the basis for some important lessons for anyone seeking to enhance the strength of a brand.

PART I
Brands and Business

1

What is a Brand?

The word 'brand' has become one of the most over-used (and misused) in the business lexicon. Given that brands are the subject of this book, it makes sense to begin by outlining what we mean by the word. So, what is a brand?

Most evidently, a brand is a name of some kind. But which kind? *Calvin Klein* is clearly a brand name, but what about *Joseph Stalin*? Certainly, lots of people have heard the name Joseph Stalin – but it would be unlikely to work as a brand of fragrances or underwear. So, what is a *brand* name? From a business perspective, we might say that a brand name is any name that is directly used to sell products or services. In addition to the name, a brand almost always has a visual expression: a symbol of some kind, a design, a trademark, a logo. Thus, the standard definition of a brand usually runs along these lines:

> *A brand is a name and/or symbol that is directly used to sell products or services.*

But surely a brand can do more than sell stuff? A strong brand, we believe, may play a broader strategic role within a business. As well as commanding market share, strong brands may create options for growth, attract and retain talented employees, and promote shareholder value. In this book, we outline the role a brand may play within a business, creating value for all stakeholders – customers, shareholders, and employees. Our definition of a brand is as follows:

> *A brand is a name and/or symbol that is used by an organization to create value for its stakeholders.*

But surely a brand is more than just a name and a visual representation? Many other things make up a brand – ranging from the stories associated with it, to the types of people who use it, to the types of places you can buy it, and even its price. In many ways, the best definition of a brand was given back in 1955 by Gardner and Levy:

> *It is a complex symbol that represents a variety of ideas and attributes. It tells the consumer many things, not only by the way it sounds (and its literal meaning if it has one) but, more important, via the body of associations it has built up and acquired as a public object over a period of time.*[1]

We believe this definition remains in many ways unsurpassed, although many have added insights and perspectives. Stephen King famously wrote, 'A product is something that is made, in a factory; a brand is something that is bought, by a consumer'. Of course, it's possible to get entangled in detailed arguments about the definition of brands. For the moment, we have identified two simple themes that we think are essential to an understanding of brands.

BRAND THEMES

1. A brand is the result of behaviour

The comedian's maxim applies here: *don't tell 'em you're funny, make 'em laugh*. Brands are judged by their actions, and not just their advertising – for a consumer, a single bad experience can unravel the most carefully spun brand. Everything a company does has the potential to impact the brand. The culture of the corporation, together with the overall strategic direction of the business, should be aligned to achieve a brand that truly resonates with stakeholders.

---

[1] Gardner and Levy, 'The product and the brand', *Harvard Business Review*, March–April 1955.

Brands are what they are because of all the ways in which they behave, both operationally and in relation to their customers . . . [A brand is] the consequence of organizational behaviours.

Adam Stagliano and Damian O'Malley[2]

[A brand is] a promise you make and keep in every marketing activity, every action, every corporate decision, every customer interaction.

Kritsin Zhivage

2. A brand exists only in people's minds

It's very easy to overlook a fundamental fact about brands: *people* bring brands to life – not companies. Brands aren't to be found in the factory or in the studio, and much less on the balance sheet – but in the minds of consumers, employees, suppliers, and others stakeholders. In a sense, a brand is a *public object* – and the strongest brands are those whose stakeholders feel a real sense of ownership: 'that's my brand'.

A brand is simply a collection of perceptions in the mind of the consumer.

Paul Feldwick

The way people build brands is in their heads. We build an image as birds build nests – from scraps and straws we chance upon.

Jeremy Bullmore

A good example of these themes in action is a newspaper. A newspaper's brand is obviously the result of behaviour: the kind of stories and photos chosen, the choice of headlines and use of language – all of this result from the daily activities of the newspaper's journalists and editors. Readers and non-readers alike form an impression of the newspaper – even those who have never even picked it up will have ideas about the kind of people who read it. Of course, those regular readers who buy it daily will tell you, 'that's my paper'.

---

[2] A. Stagliano and D. O'Malley, 'Giving up the ghost in the machine', in M. Earls and M. Baskin (eds), *Brand New Brand Thinking*, Kogan Page, 2002.

The newspaper's brand aligns its writers with its readers. The daily production of a newspaper is a complex system of judgements and values – style, presentation of facts, comment, etc. The brand provides those working on the newspaper with a shared understanding of the newspaper's 'stance' towards the news, and towards its readers.

2

Brand Strategy is Business Strategy

For a brand to really yield value, it must be more than merely the 'image' of the company, or the 'positioning' of the product: the brand must be a uniting force throughout the organization, providing the business with direction and purpose. So, what is brand strategy? Before we can reach an answer to this question, we must disentangle ourselves from some confusions and misconceptions.

BRAND STRATEGY IS MORE THAN MARKETING

Traditionally, brands are seen as a tool to achieve marketing objectives, such as growing market share, or increasing repeat purchase. Consequently, branding is seen primarily as a marketing discipline: for example, a brand can grow market share by providing a focus for awareness of a product; and it can increase repeat purchase by building affinity with consumers. Of course, a brand can play these roles, but a brand strategy is *more* than marketing.

To achieve a really powerful brand sometimes takes real guts and commitment – and often some hard decisions. Unless a brand strategy is fully aligned with the overall business strategy, it will probably fail. The following case study demonstrates that a successful brand requires more than just a good marketing effort.

Case: Continental and United

In the US major airlines such as Continental and United launched new subsidiary brands in an attempt to counter the onslaught of the budget carrier Southwest Airlines. Continental launched *Continental Lite* and United launched *Shuttle by United* – both seeking to match Southwest's short haul offer: low fares, no frills, less waiting around, and more flights.

The marketing departments of Continental and United duly delivered spectacular launches for these new brands. There was widespread national media coverage, and hundreds of people turned up to airport launch events. The prospects for these new budget airlines looked good: a successful big-bang launch into an increasingly price-sensitive industry – yet both of these start-ups have since been scrapped, while Southwest is as successful as ever. What went wrong?

Southwest is successful because its entire business is aligned with its brand position: fast, inexpensive, convenient flying. For example, fast-turnarounds are crucial to delivering this, and the airline's ground crews are highly motivated and very efficient: they're well paid and have flexible working conditions. Continental and United were unable to match this productivity: both have a highly unionized workforce with lower pay and inflexible job structures.

In all areas of their business, Continental and United were structured as a large full-service airline. Without aligning the brand and business strategy, no amount of good marketing could make a success of their new subsidiary brands.

So, what is brand strategy? A brand may have real marketing muscle behind it, but unless the efforts of the company are aligned behind it, it may fail. It's like a maxim of martial arts: a good punch comes from the body, not just from the arms. Putting together a brand strategy can involve asking some difficult questions, and ensuring that all relevant business operations support the brand position.

BRAND STRATEGY IS MORE THAN COMMUNICATIONS

To communicate is 'to impart information or ideas' – simply put, it's about getting your message across.[1] In business, it's the good old-fashioned art of persuasion: 'we' need 'them' to think or feel whatever they need to think or feel in order to do whatever it is 'we' want 'them' to do (usually, buy something).

This logic has been applied to brands, often with much success: if we want them to buy our yoghurt, our communications might contain images of health and vitality – and so people feel good about eating it, because everyone feels that he or she should be healthy and vital. If we want them to smoke our cigarettes, we can communicate with images of rugged masculinity, and so men will buy them because they enjoy this association. This is elementary branding: constructing an image that resonates in some way with the consumers, putting them in mind to buy.

However, a brand strategy is more than the blueprint for a brand image: building a strong brand takes more than communications. An enduring brand is more than the right imagery, the right tone of voice: a brand is more than what you say, it's what you do.

Case: BP – Beyond Petroleum

In 2000, BP launched a $7 million new logo together with a communications offensive to introduce *Beyond Petroleum* – the company's claim to be leading the world into a new age of cleaner energy. The strategy for the brand was in line with the company's business objectives. Firstly, BP wanted to support the growth of retail operations by strengthening its consumer brand. Secondly, having recently been through some major mergers, BP wanted the brand to create a strong sense of common purpose among its 100000 employees.

In order to deliver on this strategy, BP needed more than just communications. In such a highly sensitive (and highly scrutinized)

---

[1] Definition from *The American Heritage® Dictionary of the English Language*, Fourth Edition, Copyright © 2000 by Houghton Mifflin Company. Published by Houghton Mifflin Company. All rights reserved.

industry, BP must ensure that the rhetoric is matched by a real commitment to raising environmental standards. This means changing some attitudes and practices that are deeply ingrained within the industry – and BP have made a good start, investing in research into alternative fuels, and cutting emission levels.

Beyond Petroleum is a brave strategy for BP, risking accusations of hypocrisy if actions don't quite match rhetoric. Indeed, Greenpeace, Friends of the Earth and Corporate Watch all keep a list of environmental grievances against BP, accusing the company of 'greenwash'. BP recognizes there is still a long way to go, but most observers recognize the company is moving in the right direction. As the slogan for the *Beyond Petroleum* launch campaign put it, 'It's a start'.

So, what is brand strategy? No matter how carefully crafted a brand's communications are, sometimes it only takes one negative story – or one bad customer experience – and the whole house comes tumbling down. Brand strategy is about ensuring that what a company communicates should be aligned with what the company delivers. Put another way, a brand strategy should guarantee that the company builds its house on rock, and not sand.

BRAND STRATEGY IS MORE THAN EFFECTIVENESS

The imperative to deliver profit growth has led to a drive for operational efficiencies in all areas of business. This search for effectiveness has been the pre-occupation of much recent business activity.

Of course, any well-run business will pursue effectiveness across all of its operations: eliminating waste is essential to maintaining competitiveness, and when times are tough it can be the only way to survive. However, effectiveness – doing something *well* – is not in itself a strategy.

Brand strategy is more than effectiveness. Achieving a lift in certain brand metrics may be an indicator that a strategy is on track, but it isn't a strategic objective. For example, a campaign may lead to a growth in sales – but may simultaneously undermine the company's long-term competitive position.

Case: DHL, FedEx and UPS

By 2002, the leading players in the international air express business all shared common core propositions, namely speed (we get it there fast), reliability (we definitely get it there), and accessibility (we tell you where it is, etc.). Any innovation quickly spread across the industry, making it difficult to sustain a competitive advantage.

To compensate for this lack of differentiation, each of the leading players had extensive ongoing marketing activities. The fight now centred on who had the most attractive brand position, and the advertising featured humour, or hero-couriers, or smart 'new-economy' entrepreneurs. These campaigns were often highly effective at getting across the key messages: we're fast, we're reliable, we're accessible.

It soon became clear, however, that for the air express companies, effectiveness was having a negative side-effect. Customers became convinced that each of these companies could provide a fast, reliable service – these propositions became merely the expected level of service: customers increasingly made their purchasing decisions based upon price. For DHL, FedEx and UPS, effectiveness had turned their industry into a commodity business.

These companies have all since reviewed their brand strategies, positioning themselves as essential to operational efficiency (if the spare part doesn't arrive on time, the factory grinds to a halt). They've moved into areas such as logistics and supply-chain management – fast-developing areas where it's easier to deliver greater value to customers. As DHL puts it, 'we don't just move boxes, we move business'.

So, *what is brand strategy?* There are two things we can add to our definition. Firstly, a brand strategy must set out a credible difference from competitors. Secondly, that competitive difference must be sustainable over the longer term. Effectiveness, of course, is essential – but it is most useful as a short term indicator of performance, and rarely tells us anything about longer term trends. To use a militaristic metaphor, effectiveness is about the battle; brand strategy is about winning the war.

BRAND STRATEGY IS MORE THAN POSITIONING

The above example from DHL, UPS and FedEx demonstrates the importance of defining a sustainable difference from competitors. This is often referred to as *positioning*: the art of finding a *space* in consumers' heads.

Positioning is about clearly differentiating the brand from competitors: find the gap, and then fill it. For example, in the early 1970s the perfume manufacturer Revlon wanted to launch a new fragrance. The category was dominated by delicate, feminine brands – and so, in a bid to find a unique position, Revlon launched its *Charlie* brand. In the age of women's lib and trouser-suits, this playfully boyish position resonated with consumers – and within four years of launch *Charlie* was the world's best selling perfume.

Positioning is a useful way of thinking about branding – so much so that *positioning* and *branding* have almost become synonyms of each other. Usually, when people talk about branding, they focus on the points of difference. However, branding is about more than creating a unique position. Brand strategy is *more* than brand positioning: there are a few fundamentals that need to be addressed before a positioning can be meaningfully achieved. These are neatly illustrated in the story of the dotcom bubble.

Case: The dotcom Boom and Bust

At the height of the dotcom boom, establishing a brand position occupied much of the energy – and budget – of many new economy start-ups. A read through the archives of the marketing press reveals the almost feverish efforts with which dotcom companies sought to build strong dotcom brands, giving large budgets and equity deals to the industry's top agencies, and creating a new breed of brand consultants. In the new economy gold rush, a strong brand position seemed to be essential for grabbing market territory.

History, however, has clearly shown that brand positioning is not enough: the best brains and biggest budgets couldn't save many of these dotcoms from their fate. What went wrong? Too often, these companies focused on brand positioning, and overlooked some other essential elements of brand strategy. There are three clear lessons we can draw from the dotcom successes and failures.

1. Don't overlook awareness

In their eagerness to communicate their brand positions, many dotcoms left their potential customers in a state of some confusion about what was actually being offered. Those companies that endured are those which began with a simple, straightforward offering. Amazon.com, for example, set out with a very clear message: we sell books. Yahoo! began as a simple directory of websites, and has now built a large business around this. The most striking example is Hotmail.com, which began with hardly any communications, but became successful by offering a service – e-mail – which grew by recommendation.

2. Parity is as important as difference

The search for unique competitive positions often led many dotcoms to neglect the importance of *parity*. For example, many of the internet banks launched whacky brand positions with off-beat names and logos, eager to stand apart from the staid, impersonal services offered by the old high street banks. These new banks were beacons of new economy branding – but the bulk of customers were slow to move. Although they successfully established points of difference, appearing to be smart, accessible and flexible, they underestimated the importance of points of parity – in this case, stability, security, and integrity. In terms of parity, the old banks held their ground.

3. Make sure you can deliver

Many of the most entertaining stories from the dotcom crash come from the European clothes retailer Boo.com – and also many of the most salutary lessons. Boo.com has become a poster-child for the excesses of the dotcom period – more of a carnival than a business, fuelled by lavish parties and brainstorms in exotic locations. The founders painstakingly developed their brand position, going so far as to fly in top hairstylists by Concorde to advise on the styling of their brand mascot, Miss Boo. A vast advertising budget was effective in driving considerable numbers of potential customers to the website – but they would quickly become frustrated by poor technology, which was unable to deal with the volume of traffic. The full story of Boo's demise illustrates a multitude of business sins, but the failure to deliver was the greatest.

So, what is brand strategy? Many people regard positioning as the heart of branding – but brand strategy is more than creating a credible difference from competitors. A comprehensive strategy for a brand will ensure that consumers have a full understanding of the products or services being offered, and that points of parity with competitors are fully addressed.

BRAND STRATEGY IS BUSINESS STRATEGY

Having disentangled ourselves from some potential misconceptions, we can now return to the question: What *is* brand strategy? Any brand strategy should answer the following four questions:

1. Who are our customers?
2. What products or services will we offer?
3. How will we compete with products or services from competitors?
4. What resources and capabilities do we need to deliver these products or services?

For example, a broad articulation of the brand strategy for Southwest Airlines might read something like this:

Brand Strategy for Southwest Airlines
We will offer short-haul no-frills low-fare flights to customers who want fast, inexpensive, convenient flying. Our highly motivated employees will deliver a faster, cheaper, better service than competitors by working as a highly effective team, all with a sense of fun.

Southwest's strategy was evidently successful – it clearly had robust answers to the four brand strategy questions posed above (however they were articulated). All of the elements are closely aligned to the airlines' overall brand position: fast, inexpensive, convenient flying. In a sense, the brand has become an organizing principle for the business – galvanizing the efforts of the company behind its proposition to customers.

This, we believe, is the role of a brand strategy: to create value for a business by aligning its activities with its offering to customers. With a clear, strong brand strategy, a company may offer products and services across a range of different sectors. The Virgin brand, for example, ranges over an airline, a mobile operator, financial services, and several retail and entertainment businesses. So what is the brand strategy for Virgin? We might articulate it something like this:

Brand Strategy for Virgin

We will offer a wide range of products and services to consumers who seek quality and value for money. We will do this by challenging conventions – finding smarter, brighter ways to do things than our competitors.

This description is based upon an interview given by Virgin's boss, Richard Branson,[2] and it broadly answers the four brand strategy questions above. In simple terms, it sets out the basis for the entire Virgin business empire, aligning the activities of the various companies behind a clear mandate. The same approach can be applied to non-profit organizations: a brand strategy for the WWF (formerly the World Wildlife Fund for Nature) might read as follows:

Brand Strategy for WWF

We will promote the welfare of wildlife everywhere in the world, with the support of our donors. Instead of confrontational campaigning, we will work constructively with governments and businesses.

---

[2] BBC Money Programme, 1999.

As well as providing clear direction about what to do, a brand strategy should tell us what *not* to do. WWF, for example, resists calls to use its influence to campaign on human health issues, preferring to maintain a clear position as an environmental pressure group. Similarly, Southwest would never launch a full service, long-haul operation. Richard Branson has stated many times that Virgin will only move into areas where it can effectively challenge conventions. Some of these decisions can be hard. Sometimes, they involve saying 'no' to short-term revenue opportunities. But, as Michael Porter reminds us, 'the essence of strategy is choosing what *not* to do'.[3]

DEFINITIONS OF STRATEGY

- Strategy is a major organizational plan for action to reach a major organizational objective.
  James M. Higgins and Julian W. Vincze, *Strategic Management, Text and Cases*. Dryden Press (Chicago), 1989.
- Strategy is a plan, or something equivalent – a direction, a guide or course of action into the future, a path to get from here to there, etc. Strategy is also a pattern, that is, consistency in behavior over time.
  Henry Mintzberg, *The Rise and Fall of Strategic Planning*. The Free Press (Simon & Schuster Inc.), 1994.
- Strategy is the creation of a unique and valuable position, involving a different set of activities. . . . 'The essence of strategic positioning is to choose activities that are different from rivals'.
  Michael E. Porter, 'What is strategy?', *Harvard Business Review*, November–December 1996.
- A strategy is an integrated and coordinated set of commitments and actions designed to exploit core competencies and gain a competitive advantage.
  Michael A. Hitt, R. Duane Ireland, S. Michael Camp and Donald L. Sexton, 'Strategic entrepreneurship: entrepreneurial strategies for

---

[3] Michael E. Porter, 'What is Strategy?', *Harvard Business Review*, November–December 1996.

wealth creation', *Strategic Management Journal*, Vol. 22, June/July, pp. 479–491, 2001.

- Every organization operates on a Theory of the Business. . . . Strategy converts this Theory of the Business into performance. Its purpose is to enable an organization to achieve its desired results in an unpredictable environment. For strategy allows an organization to be purposefully opportunistic.

Peter Drucker, *Management Challenges for the 21st Century*. Butterworth-Heinemann, 1999.

3

Brands in the Boardroom

> *'The fundamental task of today's CEO is simplicity itself: Get the stock price up. Period'.*[1]

Shareholder value is the driving imperative of modern business. It wasn't always thus – and many argue that there are long-term shortfalls of the exclusive focus on capital markets. Still, this is the current business reality: top managers who want to keep their jobs must create shareholder value.

In this light, the high-flown concepts of marketing often seem far removed from real boardroom concerns. Market share and customer loyalty aren't goals in their own right. Employee satisfaction is only a means to an end. Similarly, strong brands are not an objective, but a strategy: their value lies in the ability to create value for shareholders.

Marketing sometimes seems disconnected from finance. However, senior managers do increasingly appreciate the importance of brands. A number of developments in recent years have underlined this. Some examples include:

- Strongly branded businesses command ever-higher prices at acquisition (e.g. Groupe Danone's acquisition of Nabisco Europe – see p. 151)
- Brands are playing an important role in companies recovering from bankruptcy (e.g. WorldCom's use of the MCI brand – see p. 149)

---

[1] 'The CEO Trap', *Business Week*, 11 December 2000, pp. 48–59.

Developments such as this have moved brands up the boardroom agenda. In addition, there's increasing evidence of a clear link between brands and shareholder value. In this book, we present the results of a study into the relationship between brand strength and key financial metrics, including shareholder returns (see p. 239). A number of other studies have been published in recent years. Some example findings include:

- Strong corporate brands can add up to 7% to a company's value in a bull market.[2]
- During the market crash of October 1997, businesses with strong brands were much faster to regain their losses.[3]

A link between brands and shareholder value is clear. How do we explain this? The most important driver of shareholder value is *cash flow* – the amount of cash coming into a business, after costs and investments. Brands can build shareholder value by growing and protecting a company's cash flows. In this book we will argue that strong brands harness strong cash flow for a number of reasons.

In Part II we look in detail at the specific ways in which brands create financial value for businesses – from building market share and customer loyalty, to launching into new business areas and country markets. All of these add value because they have a positive impact on the business's cash flow.

IMPACT ON CASH FLOW

Brands increase the level of cash flow

Strong brands are able to command greater market share (see p. 23) and in some cases may also command premium prices (see p. 60). Brands may also reduce the sensitivity of purchasers to changes in price (see p. 51). Strong, well-defined brands may find it easier to access

---

[2] Jeffrey Parkhurst, 'Leveraging brand to generate value', in *From Ideas to Assets: Investing Wisely in Intellectual Property*, Bruce Berman (ed.), NY: John Wiley & Sons, 2002.
[3] Russ Banham, 'Making your mark', CFO **14** (3), 34–44, 1998.

new country markets and business areas (see pp. 39 and 32). By providing a clear sense of purpose for an organization, brands may help to increase productivity and thus boost cash flow (for example, see p. 45).

Brands accelerate cash flow

Reducing the 'lag' between making an investment and enjoying the cash returns can help to boost shareholder value. Strong brands are able to launch new products and services faster than weaker brands – existing levels of awareness and trust accelerates consumers' acceptance (see p. 32). There is even reason to believe that strong brands may help to stimulate innovation – which will speed up the return of investment in product development.

Brands extend the duration of cash flow

If a brand can be maintained over the long term it becomes a 'cash cow' – a fairly low-investment source of cash flows. This isn't to suggest that maintaining a brand is easy (see p. 125), but strong brands are more likely to enjoy enduring levels of customer loyalty (see p. 71).

Brands reduce the risk attached to future cash flow

Perhaps the greatest impact brands have is in reducing the risk of cash flows and hence the value of these cash flows, which in turn creates greater shareholder returns. Strong brands have been shown to lower the inherent risk in a business (see p. 241), and may help companies to deal with disruptions to their markets (see p. 66). Brands can also create barriers to entry for competitors, thus reducing the competitive threat to cash flows (see p. 29).

Shareholder value is the language of the boardroom. Unless the case for brands is put in this language, their business potential may remain unexploited.

PART II
Sources of Business Value

4

Strong Brands Command Market Share

Source of Business Value: Brands help businesses build and maintain market share — and therefore profits

IN CONVERSATION

Time and time again, in category after category, we see the same pattern: the closer consumers get to a brand, the more likely that brand is to grow market share.

Andy Farr, Head of R&D, Millward Brown

For us, market share is the route to profitability – and our brands are the route to market share. That's why, for Unilever, investing in our brands is a strategic priority.

Niall FitzGerald, CEO, Unilever

Big, famous brands give people reassurance . . . consumers feel a sense of safety in numbers. That's partly why strong brands have stable market shares.

Mark Earls, Ogilvy & Mather

Building – and maintaining – market share is an objective for every business. There is a direct link between market share and profitability: research shows that, on average, brands with a market share of 40% generate three times the return on investment than brands with a market share of only 10% (see Figure 4.1). For many people, building or

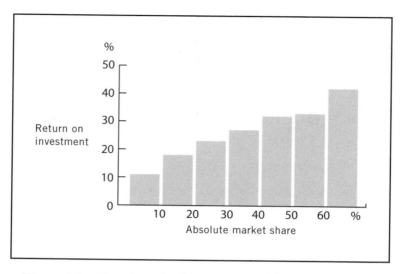

Figure 4.1 *The relationship between market share and profitability*[1]

maintaining market share – and thus, profits – is the *raison d'être* of brands.
Strong brands mean strong profits.

DEFINING MARKET SHARE

Economists and marketers mean slightly different things when they use
the word *market*. In economics, the word refers to all of the buyers and
sellers who transact particular products. For marketers, however, a market
is defined as all of the potential *buyers* for a particular product. A brand's
market share, then, is the proportion of total purchases of a particular
product accounted for by that brand.

So, *who* are the potential buyers of a brand? How do we define the market
for a particular product? This question – the touchstone of all marketing –
must obviously be answered before market share can be measured.
However, answering it may not be as simple as it first appears. Of course,
any business wants to sell as many products to as many people as possible:
it's tempting to cast the net wide and define the market in very broad terms.
However, defining the market is a key strategic issue and sometimes
involves drawing some clear boundaries – we explore these fully in Part III.

---

[1] Robert D. A. Buzzell and Bradley T. Gale, *The PIMS Principles: Linking strategy to performance*, Free Press, 1987.

Table 4.1 Strong brands have greater market share

Airlines	0.911
Banking	0.937
Beers	0.958
Cat Food	0.852
Hotels	0.758
Newspapers	0.939
Sports Good	0.872

Correlation between brand strength measures and market share (*source*: WPP's Brandz)

BRAND STRENGTH IS CORRELATED WITH MARKET SHARE

Gaining market share – and keeping it – is often seen as the *raison d'être* of branding. From the point of view of most marketers, business is the battle for market territory, and the most successful businesses seem to be those with the strongest brands. A brief look at correlations between brand strength measures and market share confirms that strong brands do indeed command market share (see Table 4.1). But what is the role of the brand in achieving this share?

THE ROLE OF A BRAND IN BUILDING MARKET SHARE: THE CASE OF INTEL

In 1989, when Intel set out to build a strong end-customer brand, the company encountered considerable scepticism. The semiconductor chip industry was regarded as a commodity market, with a standardized set of products. Competition was based upon price and performance. End-customers, according to commentators at the time, just weren't interested in chip technology: 'Most people who buy computers don't even know that the chip is in there. They care about performance. It really doesn't matter what the chip is.'[2]

Since the birth of the personal computer industry in the late 1970s, marketing had been driven by computer vendors such as IBM, Apple and Compaq, and also by software publishers such as Microsoft. The idea of a major communications push to computer buyers about a component part was radical. As Intel's own archives record, 'clearly, marketing directly to the end user was a novel idea for a semiconductor company . . . Even to many within the company, the program seemed like a stretch.'[3]

Many questioned the need for such an approach. As the campaign began, Intel was already market leader, with an impressive 56% share.[4] However, the industry was experiencing accelerating rates of change – a phenomenon that came to be known as 'Moore's law', after Intel co-founder George Moore.[5] Despite its lead, Intel could not take its competitive position for granted: 'A stronger brand was needed to separate Intel from the pack.'[6]

In 1991, after some successful US regional tests, Intel launched its landmark 'Intel Inside' programme upon the world, and by 2001, the company had invested an estimated $5.5 billion in it.[7] Available to all computer makers, the programme offered to cooperatively share costs for advertising that included the Intel branding. It was widely adopted: with almost 2000 partners, up to 90% of all PC advertising in 2001 carried the 'Intel Inside' logo.

The plunge of PC prices during the mid-1990s further fuelled consumer demand, and the consumer base broadened into a mainstream market. Many first-time computer buyers found Intel a reassuring, recognized brand. This, combined with Intel's long-standing low-margin commitment to 'price the market', was effective in securing a dominant market share: by 2001, Intel's market share was 86%.

---

[2] Quoted in Tobi Elkin and Bradley Johnson, 'Co-op Crossroads Inside Intel', *Advertising Age*, 11/99.

[3] www.intel.com.

[4] See footnote 3.

[5] Moore's law states that the number of transistors on a microprocessor roughly doubles every 18 months to two years.

[6] www.intel.com.

[7] See footnote 3.

Figure 4.2 Intel: 'a strong brand was necessary to separate Intel from the pack'

MARKET SHARE CAN BECOME SELF-REINFORCING

Nothing, the saying goes, succeeds like success. Brands with high market share are often more popular precisely because they're more popular. Big brands signal low-risk and high acceptance: consumers feel a sense of safety in numbers. In the case of Intel, the brand's strong market position became self-reinforcing. When the mainstream PC market was very young, consumers wanted guidance and reassurance. In other words, everybody wanted Intel inside because everybody else had Intel inside.

This effect can be seen across many categories – even those in which we might assume the decision-making process is highly rational, such as pharmaceutical brands. Studies into doctors' prescribing practices show that market share has a significant influence on the choice of brand.[8] Any brand which achieves a leading market share may find its position consolidated in this way – intensifying the challenge for smaller brands.

OTHER FACTORS CONTRIBUTE TO MARKET SHARE

It's a common pattern across categories: the market leader has the strongest brand. However, the strength of the brand may not always be

---

[8] W. Desarbo *et al.*, 'Gravity-based multidimensional scaling model for deriving spatial structures underlying consumer preference/choice judgments'. *Journal of Consumer Research (USA)*, June 2002, Online.

the determining factor. People may buy Microsoft because of the brand, but the majority of the company's sales are the result of structural factors, such as the preloading of software onto its operating systems.

For a number of categories, a strong brand is not the most important factor. In the airline industry, for example, market share is determined primarily by a combination of price, route and schedule; frequent flier programmes also act to reinforce customer behaviours by feeding their appetite for air miles. Brand preferences may exist, but they alone do not drive purchase.

VALUE CHECK

- What market are you in?

- What market are you NOT in?

- Question your answers to the above two questions.

5

Strong Brands Create Barriers to Entry for Competitors

Source of Business Value: Brands can discourage potential competitors from entering a market

IN CONVERSATION

In a world where it takes less than 6 months on average to replicate any true product innovation, a brand is often the only barrier to competition.

Steve Hayden, Ogilvy & Mather

If a brand is really strong – strong enough to really stand for something in consumers' heads – then it's harder for competitors to present a credible alternative.

Tony Wright, Ogilvy & Mather

If a business is harvesting healthy profits from a particular industry, new firms typically enter the market to take advantage of the high profit levels. Over time, this typically drives down profitability for all companies in the industry, and may also erode market share for the original players. Guarding against new entrants is a strategic priority for successful businesses.

Investment in a brand may be part of a strategy to create barriers to entry for potential competitors. Industry-specific characteristics often make it difficult for a company to freely enter a market. For example, the minimum level of production that would be cost-efficient may be higher than the level of sales a new entrant could expect. Strong brands may act as an effective barrier to entry for potential competitors. This can work in two ways.

BRAND ADVERTISING IS A SUNK COST

Soap powder is very cheap to produce, using low-level technology. So why is the soap powder market dominated for long periods by a small number of brands? Incumbent brands spend heavily on advertising – precisely in order to create a barrier to entry. If a new soap powder brand wants to persuade customers to switch, it would need to at least match the spending of the incumbents. In the UK the advertising cost of a launch for a soap powder brand is estimated to be around £10 million – and this has been sufficient to deter new entrants.

Advertising is known as a *sunk cost* – in other words, a cost that cannot be reversed. For example, if you decide to pay £5 to go to the cinema, you're unlikely to get your money back if you don't like the film. If the cost of the ticket is very high – say £20 – you're unlikely to go unless you're very sure you're going to enjoy it. Similarly, if a company must spend a large amount on advertising in order to enter a market, it's unlikely to do so unless it's very sure of success.

An additional effect further strengthens the barrier to entry. New entrants will, of course, seek to recoup the costs of entry. However, the addition of a new player into the market will usually result in price competition. The incumbent, free from the need to recoup any cost of entry, is likely to be able to drive the price low without losing margins – and will probably win any price war.

BRAND AS AN EXCLUSIVE POSITION

There is a second way that a brand may create barriers to entry. In some markets, one brand has become so dominant that consumers associate it almost exclusively with the product or service it offers. It occupies the 'high ground', so to speak. In these cases it can be very difficult for new entrants to make any impact.

This can be seen clearly among those businesses that have developed brands from products that are in fact ingredients in another end-consumer product, such as Dolby, Intel, NutraSweet, Teflon and Lycra. This 'ingredient branding' has a dual effect: it stimulates demand for the 'host brand', and thereby grows volume, while simultaneously locking-out potential competitors.

The case of NutraSweet shows how effectively a brand can block out new entrants. Monsanto launched NutraSweet as an ingredient co-brand with Diet Coke and Wrigley's Extra, while supporting this with advertising on the benefits of NutraSweet. Not only did NutraSweet quickly become the expected standard in low-calorie soft drinks, but it is so successful that even competitors in the sweetener market, such as Canderel from Searle, are now co-branded with NutraSweet. This brand has successfully secured an exclusive position in its market – effectively deterring new entrants.

VALUE CHECK

- Imagine you are a potential new entrant into your market.
  - What are the top three reasons to enter?
  - What are the top three reasons not to enter?

- Imagine a new entrant has come into your market.
  - What's the worst case scenario?
  - How can you use your brand to deter this scenario?

6

Strong Brands Can Launch
Successful Extensions

Source of Business Value: Brands provide business with options for growth through brand extensions

IN CONVERSATION

I believe a strong brand gives you options – and launching new products or services is probably the most valuable option of all. It's a major dividend of investing in the brand.

Sir Niall FitzGerald, CEO, Unilever

Launching brand extensions is a bit like having kids – just because you *can* doesn't mean you *should*. But if the conditions are right, and everything is thoroughly prepared and thought through, then it can be terrifically rewarding.

Rory Sutherland, Creative Director, OgilvyOne

A brand that has established itself in one business area may extend into others, launching new products or services under the same brand. Brand extensions can create value for a business in a number of ways: by accessing new sources of revenue, by revitalising a brand in the eyes of the consumer, or by helping a business to respond to a significant change in the market.

BRAND EXTENSIONS CAN KEEP A BRAND UP-TO-DATE

Established brands face a particular challenge. If the brand isn't kept up-to-date and fresh, it risks losing its relevance and appeal. On the other hand, if the brand isn't consistent – if it moves too far, too fast – it risks undermining the bonds it has with existing consumers. Striking the balance between change and consistency is an ongoing issue for established brands – and launching brand extensions is one method of addressing this.

The skincare brand Pond's has been striking this balance for over 150 years. As one of the world's oldest beauty products, Pond's has had to adapt to women's changing attitudes towards beauty, while keeping the brand firmly grounded in its brand values. The launch of the *Pond's Institute* in the 1990s helped to accomplish this, giving the brand a sense of permanence and authority, as well as a sense of innovation and change. However, more than anything, Pond's has used extensions to keep its brand fresh.

For example, in the US in the late 1990s, Pond's clearly needed to reach a younger audience for the brand, without undermining its well-established consumer base. A brand extension was the solution, and Pond's developed a new product: an overnight treatment aimed for young girls suffering from mild acne. The launch campaign featured graphics by MTV's animations studio, carried on highly targeted youth media and on the Web. The product's sales were very healthy, although the extension will be considered a success if it brings younger consumers into the Pond's franchise.

BRAND EXTENSIONS CAN HELP A BUSINESS RESPOND TO MARKET CHANGES

If a market undergoes substantial change, brand extension can literally save the business. Some interesting lessons can be learned from responses to the rise of digital technologies in the 1990s – particularly from Kodak, Letraset and Encyclopaedia Britannica.

- Kodak's traditional market is photographic films – but the company recognizes the very present threat from digital photography. Indeed, Kodak has acknowledged that digital camera use has triggered a significant fall in film sales – estimated to be around 10% in 2003. However, Kodak has an extremely strong consumer brand associated with photography: anticipating the changes in its market, Kodak has already extended its brand into the digital market, offering digital cameras, display screens and photo printers.

- In 1987, the Letraset brand was synonymous with the dry-transfer lettering system that the company pioneered. However, even at the height of its success, Letraset's market was changing. The emergence of desk-top publishing has almost completely obliterated Letraset's business. Letraset were slow to respond: by the time the company moved into digital fonts its brand had come to represent out-moded technology. It could have been very different. At its peak, Letraset had a strong brand: an innovative company that had democratized typography. What better image for a digital font producer?

- Encyclopaedia Britannica's management famously disregarded the threat posed by CD-Rom and Internet technology in the 1990s. In its 230-year history the company had not experienced any significant changes in its market, so it was unprepared for the rapid, extensive changes that came with the emergence of digital technology. Sales of the encyclopaedia in North America fell from 117000 units in 1990 to 51000 in 1994. Responding to this change was an enormous challenge, and the company looked to its greatest asset: its very well-known, highly trusted brand. A number of brand extensions have kept the business viable, including CD-Roms, DVDs and numerous Internet ventures.

BRAND EXTENSIONS CAN ENABLE A BUSINESS TO ACCESS NEW REVENUE STREAMS

Companies such as Unilever and Procter & Gamble have high rates of new product introductions, using innovation to stimulate consumer spending. Traditionally, these new products would be launched with new brands. However, the marketing costs of launching new products have risen, and these companies are adopting a new strategy: concentrate advertising spend into a smaller number of big brands, and launch new products as extensions to these brands.

It's not just consumer goods companies who are exploiting brand extensions. Even the top professional sports clubs are finding that brand extensions are a common source of additional revenues. In the US the Dallas Cowboys and New York Yankees are the champions of converting fans into customers, although many sports brands stress another important objective: to foster a stronger relationship with fans through interactions with the brand. Perhaps cautious of appearing to exploit the goodwill of fans, many clubs are reluctant to talk in purely commercial terms. Not so for UK football giants Manchester United, as marketing head Peter Draper writes:

> A lot of people don't like talking about football clubs as a business – but we do. Our objective is to take the best elements of Manchester United and market them to millions of fans and millions of people.[1]

After a long period of sustained success on the field, the corporate masters of Manchester United FC faced an unusual challenge: how to convert an estimated 50 million fans worldwide into a profitable market for the Manchester United Plc. The club had become a substantial global brand, and has since franchised extensive merchandising operations world wide – there is even a French Connection style clothing label, *mufc*. Among the many ventures is a TV channel, *MUTV*, and a chain of *Reds* cafés and stores in key Asian cities.

These successful brand extensions – sometimes into radically different business areas, are achievable for the big sports brands because of the high levels of customer involvement. As Peter Draper puts it, 'they give us their hearts and their souls'. However, when Manchester United

---

[1] Quoted in *Uncommon Practice*, edited by Andy Milligan and Shaun Smith, Interbrand/FT Prentice Hall, 2002.

launched a children's red toothpaste, many thought things were getting out of hand. As the *Financial Times* commented, 'What will United think of next? Fabien Barthez anti-dandruff shampoo? Laurent Blanc anti-ageing cream?'[2]

BRAND STRENGTH DOESN'T GUARANTEE SUCCESSFUL BRAND EXTENSION

Brand strength alone isn't enough to guarantee successful brand extensions. Even the strongest of brands risk going too far when moving into new areas. In 1995 Procter & Gamble extended their *Olay* skincare brand into cosmetics, only to announce an about-turn in 2001. Consumer response hadn't been as strong as intended: the company had planned for a minimum 7% market share in the US, and had achieved barely 3%. Unilever was forced to pull the plug on its brand extension project for *Domestos* in the UK: after two years of product launches – bathroom mousse, surface wipes, etc. – the brand has been restored to its roots: a toilet cleaning bleach.

BRAND STRENGTH CAN OCCASIONALLY BE A HINDRANCE TO BRAND EXTENSION

Each of these failed brand extensions rested upon the assumption that the brand's strength in one category could give it access to another area of business. In some cases brand strength may even be a hindrance. In the UK, for example, the AA (Automobile Association) is a very powerful brand, well known and trusted among motorists. Attempts by the AA to move into other areas – such as personal finance – have had to overcome these strong associations. An AA spokeswoman summed it up: "AA

---

[2] Quoted by Wyn Grant in his fan's website http://members. tripod.com/ ~WynGrant/ManUtd.html.

membership is a very powerful brand but it does have the effect of eclips-ing the other products that we have.'[3]

BRAND EXTENSIONS MAY DAMAGE THE CORE BRAND POSITION

In the same way that brand extension can be used to up-date and refresh a brand, there is always a risk that an extension may in some way damage the brand. Businesses that operate low-volume premium brands may seek to cash in on the brand's strength by launching down-market brand extensions. This is particularly tempting for car manufacturers such as BMW and Mercedes, who are always attempting to exploit their prestige marques with mainstream audiences. However, the risk of this approach is that it may erode the premium value inherent in the core brand.

For example, in the 1970s Porsche's marketers identified the need for a less costly, entry-level Porsche – and so in 1977 the Porsche 924 was launched. All of Porsche's previous models had been born of a genuine dedication to the pure performance sports car niche, and the resulting high quality gave Porsche's brand its strength. As a low-cost model, the 924 couldn't match these standards. To car lovers, it seemed to mark the end of the Porsche legend. Porsche responded by raising both the quality and the price of the 924 – the company's official line now is that the only entry-level Porsche is a used Porsche.

---

[3] Rebecca Hadley, quoted in Morag Cuddeford, 'Over-stretching the brand', *Brand Strategy*, May 2002.

VALUE CHECK

- Imagine that your lead product or service ceased to exist. How would you use your brand?

- List three new products that would refresh the way that customers think of you.

- Evaluate the following imaginary brand extensions. Which one would you back, and why?
  - Boeing Luggage
  - Sony Theme Park
  - USAF Sunglasses
  - Mont Blanc Hotels
  - IKEA Coffee

7

Strong, Well-Defined Brands Find it Easier to Enter New Country Markets

Source of Business Value: Brands can allow businesses to access revenues by launching in new countries

The image of a brand is a subjective thing. No two people, however similar, hold precisely the same view of the same brand. That highest of ambitions for many CEOs, a global brand, is therefore a contradiction in terms and an impossibility.

Jeremy Bullmore, WPP

Our strongest brands have been very successful at establishing themselves in new markets – this has been a critical part of our growth as a company.

Sir Niall FitzGerald, Unilever

The extension of brands into new markets has become a major way in which businesses maintain their growth rates. Substantial market shares have been achieved across the world by a small number of brands, mostly of US origin. The relaxation of restrictions on international trade, together with improved logistics for transport and distribution, has made it easier for companies to create value by establishing their brands overseas.

COCA-COLA LEADS THE CHARGE

The brand most often mentioned in this connection is Coca-Cola, whose global ambition began in earnest with the entry of US forces into the Second World War. Seizing the moment, the company announced that every soldier would be able to buy a Coca-Cola for 5 cents – anywhere in the world, regardless of cost. The US Government helped to build dozens of overseas bottling plants, in the belief that Coke would be good for troop morale. It's a strong example of the enterprising response of US business to the Second World War – and Coca-Cola enjoyed a post-war surge in growth, both at home and abroad.

INTERNATIONAL BRANDS ARE FAIRLY RECENT

Apart from occasional overseas ventures, most companies were generally confined to national borders until 20 years ago – even Coca-Cola made more than two-thirds of its sales in the US until the mid-1980s. Far from aggressive extensions into new geographical markets, most US brands were preoccupied with their vast domestic market. As recently as 1985, American businesses were criticized by observers for their 'international myopia'[1]:

> The resources and marketing efforts committed to foreign markets are weak and lacking in marketing depth . . . Reluctance to undertake serious global marketing not only hurts these firms but will also ruin the nation's economy as a whole.

THE JAPANESE APPROACH

In 1985 US business was faced wtih its biggest post-war challenge: 'the Japanese export invasion', as it was called. In market after market US

---

[1] S. Jatusriptiak, L. Fahey, and P. Kotler, 'Strategic Global Marketing: Lessons from the Japanese', *Columbia Journal of World Business*, Spring 1985.

companies had seen their market shares fall, as Japanese business deployed its irresistible high-quality/low-price formula. Many strong brands were forged during this period – Sony, Honda and others – but the initial global success of Japanese business was *not* primarily a brand story: it was about superior product at a competitive price.

THE US APPROACH

Contrast this with the global march of the big US consumer brands, which reached its peak during the mid-1990s. Those brands that are most global – Marlboro, Coca-Cola, Levis, Budweiser, McDonald's, etc. – have built their success on carefully constructed brands. The leaders of these brands are proud of their brand-building prowess:

> Brand Coca-Cola is at the core of our business and brand building is our expertise.[2]
> Douglas N. Daft, Chairman/CEO of The Coca-Cola Company

> Consistency behind a sharply defined and relevant Brand Position is the critical factor behind Dove's success.[3]
> Silvia Lagnado, Dove Global Brand Director, Unilever

> Focusing on the product was a great way for a brand to start, but it wasn't enough. We had to fill in the blanks, starting with understanding who the consumer is and what the brand represents.[4]
> Phil Knight, Founder, Chairman/CEO, Nike

COUNTRY OF ORIGIN PLAYS A LARGE ROLE

Sir Martin Sorrell is quoted as saying, 'there is no globalization; there's only *Americanization*'. Some commentators attribute the success of the big

[2] Douglas N. Daft, 'Connecting with global consumers', *Executive Excellence*, October 2000.
[3] Silvia Lagnado, Unilever HPC North America presentation, 14 November 2002.
[4] Phil Knight, interview with Geraldine E. Willigan, 'High-performance marketing', *Harvard Business Review*, July–August 1992.

US brands to their American origin; Coke, for example, is said to access 'a latent demand that is present around the world . . . the appeal of American youth imagery'.[5] Many major American brands have relied upon the attractiveness of *Americana* – although this seems a precarious strategy, since resentment towards America is growing in many parts of the international consumer marketplace.

Many brands from other countries make use of their country of origin. The apparel brand Burberry, with its distinctive, signature plaid, has worldwide reach – but stays close to its British heritage. The brand has been adopted by many different cultural groups – from west-coast hip hop to Welsh football fans – but Burberry hasn't followed the example of other luxury brands by endorsing these unintended markets. Instead the company prefers to remain more traditionally British – distinctive, and slightly reserved. Sales are responding well to this approach – reaching US$711.7 million, up from US$605.9 in 2001.

The potential advantage that a brand's country of origin may bring is sufficiently large that plenty of brands are deceptive about their provenance. Saisho is a mock-Japanese electronics brand sold by UK retailer Dixons – although it is about as Japanese as Big Ben. Brooklyn is Italy's number-one selling chewing gum – it is manufactured in Milan by an Italian company, despite its US styling. For a brand seeking to establish themselves in new country markets, deciding on the role of the country of origin is a crucial first step.

TYPES OF INTERNATIONAL BRAND

Broadly speaking there are three approaches to deciding on how to position a brand with respect to its country of origin – resulting in three types of international brand:

- *The naturalized brand*: Brands that have followed this approach have 'gone native': consumers largely assume they come from their own country. Examples include Axe, Dove, Colgate and Esso.
- *The exotic brand*: These brands have capitalized on their provenance, using their country of origin to enhance the brand position. Outside

---

[5] H. Riensenbeck and A. Freeling, 'How global are global brands?', *McKinsey Quarterly*, Number 4, 1991.

of their home markets, these brands are always perceived to be 'foreign'. Examples include German cars such as Audi and BMW.

- **The ubiquitous brand**: Many brands live in a strange nowhere-land with no particular geographical underpinning. Consumers aren't sure where they come from – and don't really care. Examples include Ambre Solaire, Hilton and Lego.

A STRONG BRAND IS NOT ENOUGH

It is tempting to assume that the success of a brand in the domestic market means that success is assured in new country markets. Indeed, there are many examples that seem to support this. However, it is very easy to underestimate the impact of local, culturally-specific factors. There are many examples of strong domestic brands that have failed to establish themselves in new markets – even when those markets appear fairly similar, such as the US and UK.

In the 1980s, for example, Kellogg's had built its *Nutragrain* brand into the leading US health cereal, with no emphasis on the Kellogg's name. When the company first tried to launch the brand in the UK in 1986, it fared poorly. UK consumers were not yet as health-conscious as those in the US, and did not respond to the 'nutrition' aspect of the brand's name, or its overall health positioning. It was withdrawn from sale in the UK in 1989.

THE PENDULUM SWINGS: LOCAL VS GLOBAL

During the 1990s, the global expansion of the big, centrally managed brands seemed to stall. Increasingly, local consumers were affronted by cultural insensitivities. In March 2000, Coca-Cola announced a new 'think local, act local' marketing strategy: understanding local tastes, and acquiring local brands. This was the latest swing of the pendulum between local and global.

Approaches to international branding have become cyclical. For a period the brand may be run by a small group of god-like people, guardians of the brand's essence, keepers of manuals and guidelines, stewards of brand purity. Then the focus of activity swings to a local team, who are suddenly empowered with the freedom of budgets to engage their local consumers. In time, the pendulum swings back again.

This pattern is seen in many global brands. It's not some kind of interminable indecisiveness – rather, it is an attempt to find a balanced strategy in the face of two opposing drivers:

- *Drivers for local branding*: There is one overwhelming argument for developing brand strategies at a local level – the diversity in the global consumer marketplace. Anyone who has looked at in-depth studies of consumers across many markets will be aware of the many strange and wonderful differences between even apparently similar cultures.

- *Drivers of global branding*: On the other hand, there are two main reasons for centrally developing brand strategy.
  - We do now live in a global village – consumers are more mobile, the media has become globalized, and the internet and the euro further diminished boundaries. Consumers *expect* consistency from their brands.
  - Global branding places a central team in control – allowing quality assurance and delivering economies of scale.

VALUE CHECK

- Do your consumers value consistency across markets?

- How diverse are the global consumers of your brand?

- What is the balance of local and global drivers?

- What is the role of country of origin?

8

Strong Brands can Attract and Retain Talent

Source Of Business Value: Brands create competitive advantage by attracting talented employees – and keeping them

---

IN CONVERSATION

The first and most important audience for any company is its own employees. After all, who wants to be embarrassed when someone asks them where they work? The better the impression of the employer's brand in the outside world, the more likely it is that good people will want to work there.

Jon Steel, WPP

Recruiting, hiring and training new employees are major direct costs for most businesses. Strong brands can help to reduce these costs by raising the profile of the company and increasing its attractiveness as an employer. In addition, a strong brand may help to attract the *right kind* of candidate, because it may communicate information about the culture of the company.

Retaining talent is also a strategic priority for businesses: as well as avoiding additional recruitment costs, employees leaving a company are likely to join a competitor – taking valuable organizational knowledge. High levels of 'churn' may disrupt relationships with customers and suppliers, disrupt formation of well-functioning teams and prevent the business from moving forward.

Despite these negative impacts, levels of churn in many industries are high: 30% in London advertising agencies, with similar levels reported by major management consultancies. Fast food retailers have staff churn rates of around 60%. The cost of re-recruiting is a major factor for schools and hospitals – not to mention the negative effects of discontinuity.

Strong brands can help organizations to retain talented employees. A brand can be an articulation of an organization's sense of *purpose* – and people are more likely to remain if they believe in what the company stands for. Strong brands can engender a sense of pride and a level of emotional loyalty in staff.

As consumers, people use brands as a guide to quality, as a store of trust, and as a way of building their own social identities. As employees, people use brands as a guide to the calibre, stability and prospects of a job, and as a way of building their own professional reputations. Companies can use their 'employer brands' to attract and retain the best employees.

ATTRACTING AND RETAINING TALENT HAS BECOME A STRATEGIC PRIORITY

In the era of the job-for-life, companies didn't need to worry too much about attracting and retaining talented employees. They had a yearly intake from schools and universities, which were fed through intensive apprenticeships and training programmes. Over time these new employees would progress through the ranks of the company, often remaining loyal until it was time to collect the gold-plated carriage-clock, and draw their company pension.

But things have changed. Then, employers sought to build a stable, long-term workforce; now companies are expected to be 'lean and mean', and the priority is short-term shareholder returns. Until the 1970s, most employees expected job security, with stable pay and a predictable promotion ladder. Now most people wouldn't want a job for life – they want flexibility, diversity and independence.

In this new, dynamic employment market, attracting and retaining talent is a strategic priority for any business. As McKinsey described it, employers are engaged in 'the war for talent'.[1] In this ultra-competitive recruiting environment, many successful businesses have begun to actively explore ways in which their brand can play a role in winning the competition for talent.

BUILDING EMPLOYER BRANDS

A shift has taken place in the world of recruitment – away from the old, checklist-driven approaches to HR, which treated recruitment as a kind of procurement process, and towards a more people-focused approach, which tries to appeal to the values and aspirations of potential employees. Given that there is competition for prospective employees, it's easy to see the attraction of thinking about recruitment as a kind of marketing, rather than as a kind of purchasing.

Against this background, many organizations have begun to apply the methods of consumer branding to recruiting the best employees. This allows companies to ask questions about potential recruits:

- What are they looking for in an employer?
- How do they make employment decisions?
- What role does work play in their lives?
- What do they currently think about us?

Understanding the target audience is, of course, the starting point for any kind of branding. With consumer branding, the next step is to define the proposition: having defined our target audience, what will we offer them? With employee branding, this translates into a golden rule: *be clear about what you do*.

BE CLEAR ABOUT WHAT YOU DO

This means more than a corporate mission statement. Consider, for example, two strategic consulting firms – Boston Consulting Group

---

[1] Ed Michaels, Helen Handfield-Jones and Beth Axelrod, *McKinsey Quarterly*, Harvard Business School Press, 2001.

(BCG) and McKinsey. Both companies are very clear about what they do, and both are highly desirable employers. They each attract different types of candidates: BCG attracts people with a broad and varied experience of business, whereas McKinsey attracts 'blank slate' candidates (often recent graduates) who are looking for thorough training.[2] This reflects the different approach of the two companies: BCG clients expect that each project team will come up with a unique, innovative solution; McKinsey clients expect the rigorous application of proprietary tools and products.

Because both companies have a clear approach to their business, they find it easy to attract the right kind of candidates. Thus, BCG's website boasts 'No two paths to BCG are the same. And no two consultants are alike',[3] whereas McKinsey has a neat flow diagram showing possible career development.[4] Both companies have strong brands aligned with a strong business model: not only can they attract talent, they can attract the *right type* of talent.

MONEY ALONE ISN'T ENOUGH TO RETAIN TALENT

The factors that attract employees to a company will often determine whether or not they will stay. McKinsey recruits, for example, are likely to remain with the company to take advantage of the formal career development. BCG employees, attracted by the entrepreneurial environment, may be more likely to leave (although they often return). Employees who are attracted by financial reward alone will be most easily lured by better offers: even the most generous 'golden handcuffs' can be offset by signing bonuses. An organization that has a clear sense of identity – a strong employee brand – is more likely to keep hold of its best staff.

---

[2] For further discussion, see P. Cappelli and A. Crocker-Hefter, 'Distinctive human resources are firm's core competencies', *The War for Talent*.
[3] http://www.bcg.com/careers/careers_splash.asp
[4] http://www.mckinsey.com/careers/

DON'T OVERLOOK THE DETAILS

Consider the approach to retaining talent taken by United Parcel Service, described by Peter Cappelli in the *Harvard Business Review*. The company discovered a significant problem with the retention of their drivers – crucial to UPS, with their in-depth knowledge of local routes and customers. An investigation traced the problem to the 'tedious and exhausting' task of loading the vans at the beginning of a run. The company simply assigned this task to warehouse staff, and the turnover of drivers fell dramatically.[5] UPS is a strong brand with a proud heritage – and drivers may enjoy their vintage UPS trucks – but the solution was more about moving boxes than moving brand perceptions.

BRINGING TOGETHER MARKETING AND HR

In terms of communications, the growth of employer branding has led to the need for alignment between internal and external. Michael Pounsford of internal communications agency Banner McBride describes the need for 'a single consistent approach to both customers and employees', while Mark Ritson of the London Business School calls for 'a rare unification between marketing and HR'. It's an interesting question: in a company, *who* exactly is responsible for talent? If an organization's brand is to generate value from both customers and employees, an integrated approach is needed.

---

[5] P. Cappelli, 'A market driven approach to retaining talent', *Harvard Business Review*, Jan.–Feb. 2000.
[6] Michael Pounsford, 'Winning the war for talent', *Strategic Communications Management*, Oct.–Nov. 2001.

VALUE CHECK

- Can you describe your employer brand?

- What is your ideal employee looking for from an employer?

- Are you clear enough about what you do?

- Do new joiners think that reality matches expectation?

- How would you describe the *purpose* of your organization?

- Do marketing and HR ever talk to each other?

9

Strong Brands have Lower Price Elasticity

Source Of Business Value: Brands can support the price that a purchaser is willing to pay

IN CONVERSATION

I think that, as more markets become more competitive, the focus for brands will become about supporting the price consumers will pay for products.

Tony Wright, Ogilvy & Mather

It stands to reason – Strong brands can weather modest prices increases. But no matter how strong, every brand has a pricepoint of inflection where its emotional appeal begins to be outweighed by economic disincentives. Past that point, disaster waits.

Garth Hallberg, author of *All Consumers Are Not Created Equal*

A strong brand may be able to raise prices without losing too much sales volume. This is known in economics as *price elasticity* – the amount by which sales will change as a result of a small change in price.

- A brand has *high* price elasticity if a small increase in price leads to a large fall in sales.

- A brand has *low* price elasticity if a small increase in price leads to a small fall in sales.

Of course, all companies would like to operate in an environment where price elasticity is *low*: increasing prices without losing significant volume is obviously good for business. A brand can help to create lower price elasticity.[1]

BRAND STRATEGY IS ABOUT MORE THAN *VOLUME*

The focus of much brand strategy is *volume* – with brands cast in the role of competing empires, engaged in the conquest and defence of market territory. The frequent appearance of words like 'acquisition' and 'retention' reflect this emphasis – although it often overlooks an essential element: *price*. As Simon Broadbent puts it, 'the real benefit of branding is often less in creating volume than in supporting the price that a purchaser is ready to pay'.[2]

It is often taken for granted that the objective of brand strategy is to increase sales volumes. Marketing activities – such as advertising – are frequently conceived in terms of market share. In many ways this is a relic of the early and expansionist years of marketing, when the main challenge was to win new consumers. In fact, branding is largely a process of adding values, enabling businesses to maintain their prices.

BRAND CAMPAIGNS CAN REDUCE PRICE ELASTICITY

Investing in brand communications can reduce the sensitivity that consumers might have to changes in price. A study into a campaign by the

---

[1] The notion that stronger brands are better able to raise prices without losing volume is well-entrenched. It often is suggested that price elasticity should be taken as a measure of brand strength – see, for example, Paul Feldwick, 'What is brand equity, anyway?' WARC.

[2] Simon Broadbent, 'Diversity in categories, brands and strategies', *Journal of Brand Management*, Vol. 2(1), 1994.

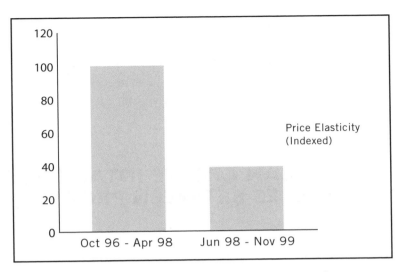

Figure 9.1 *Lurpack brand campaign reduced price elasticity*

UK butter brand Lurpack demonstrates this. For some years, the company had been maintaining an econometric model which enabled them to estimate the effects of changes in price on volumes sales – in other words, price elasticity. Figure 9.1 shows the change in elasticity estimated across two time periods. The campaign ran from 1997 to 1999. A clear reduction in price sensitivity is evident.

SOME CATEGORIES HAVE HIGHER PRICE ELASTICITY

How consumers respond to a change in price obviously depends upon the kind of commodity in question – this has been well understood for centuries. In ancient times, skilled traders such as the Phoenicians had an astute grasp of prices: they understood that the demand for some commodities (such as British tin) did not change much, even if the prices increased, while their appetite for luxury goods (such as Chinese silk or Indian spices) was very sensitive to a change in price.

In these examples, tin would be said to have *low* levels of elasticity, whereas silk and spices have *high* levels. This reflects a long-standing idea in economics that elasticity is a function of *necessity*, and this can still be seen clearly today. For instance, oil has a low level of price elasticity because people are reluctant to stop using their cars even if the price increases. Newspaper sales, on the other hand, have higher price elasticity: if the price goes up, people are more likely to pass. If levels of price elasticity are determined partly by category-specific factors, what role can brands play?

BRANDS CAN CREATE INTANGIBLE DIFFERENCES BETWEEN PRODUCTS

Many studies have been done to show that strong brands have lower price elasticity: an econometric study on the UK tea brand PG Tips, for example, shows that a 1% increase in the price of PG Tips relative to competitors leads to a drop of 0.4 market share points. The effect of a similar increase in the competitor's price is much larger: a 1% increase in Tetley's price results in a downturn of 1.4 share points. The authors take this to show the power of the brand:

> We conclude that this is further evidence of the added value of the PG Tips brand compared with its major rivals since it implies that consumers are more likely to ignore price (in favour of other 'values') when it comes to purchasing PG Tips.[3]

According to economic theory, the key to explaining this is *differentiation*. If there are many substitutes for a product, then elasticity is high – people simply switch. If no other product is quite the same, then elasticity is lower. The low price elasticity for PG Tips is explained by the fact that UK tea drinkers appear to be very particular about their brew. In the PG Tips study, the authors cite the results of taste tests. In branded tests, respondents overwhelmingly prefer PG Tips (although in blind tests, nobody can tell the difference). In the consumer's mind, at least, there's nothing quite like a cup of PG Tips.

---

[3] Clive Cooper, Louise Cook and Nigel Jones, 'How the chimps have kept PG Tips brand leader through 35 years of intense competition', *IPA*, 1990.

ULTIMATELY, IT'S THE PRODUCT THAT COUNTS

The PG Tips case clearly shows that branding can create differentiation where little exists, thereby achieving lower price elasticity. However, influencing price through branding alone can be a precarious strategy: ultimately, it's the product that counts. When, in 1999, Coca-Cola calculated that elasticity was sufficiently low to sustain a 5% rise in price, it did not foresee the recall of 17 million cases in Europe. The company had estimated that a slightly lower volume at a higher price would yield increased earnings, but in the event the price rise led to a far greater fall in volume than expected.

The Coca-Cola case illustrates a central point in our discussion on brands: the product is king. As Jeremy Bullmore reminds us, 'you can't, of course, produce a successful brand without producing a good product first'.[4] The surest way to achieve brand differentiation is *product innovation*. Successful innovation pushes products out of the range of any substitutes, thus lowering price elasticity: because consumers cannot easily switch to an alternative, they become less responsive to price rises.

Companies such as Gillette have used product innovation to neutralize competitors – for many of its consumers, the alternative to a Gillette product is a beard. Gillette extensively tested the price elasticity of its Mach3 razor blade before launch in 1993, and discovered that elasticity was so low that they were able to push the price to 35% more than its predecessor, the Sensor. Such low levels of elasticity are often taken to be a sign that a *de facto* monopoly is forming, and innovation-led companies such as Gillette, Boeing and Xerox have all attracted the attention of government competition regulators.

BIG BRANDS HAVE LOWER PRICE ELASTICITY

Levels of price elasticity change according to how *big* a brand is. For example, a study into prices of liquor in the US shows that consumers of

---

[4] Jeremy Bullmore, in WPP Annual Report & Accounts, 2000.

brands with high market share are far less responsive to changes in price than consumers of smaller brands.[5] This is a kind of 'double jeopardy' effect: small brands are punished not only by lower market share, but by higher price elasticity.

BRANDS CAN OCCASIONALLY 'CHEAT' PRICE ELASTICITY

People's response to changes in price is not always rational and linear – and companies can exploit this. For example, a drop in price from £2.00 to £1.99 is likely to have a greater effect than a drop from £1.99 to £1.98. A series of gradual price rises will have less negative effect on volume than a single large rise – although the final price may be the same. Also, a rise in price may lead to an *increase* in demand, if price is used as a guide to quality – an issue which we explore elsewhere in this section (see p. 61).

THE CASE OF MARLBORO FRIDAY

For many years, Philip Morris placed its faith in the strength of the Marlboro brand. The company was convinced that – bolstered by strong brand communications – price elasticity could be kept low enough to sustain a prolonged period of incremental price rises. These price rises, sometimes as high as 4% above inflation, continued until 1993, by which time a full-priced pack of Marlboro cost over $2, while generic, own-label products sold for as little as 69 cents.

Philip Morris, like most businesses, was intent on pushing its price to the limits of the market. In the process, it had opened up a large gap at the price-sensitive end of market consumption – and the generic products were there to exploit it. As Marlboro continued to push its prices, these virtually unbranded products worked hard to increase quality, and

---

[5] Francis J. Mulhern and Jerome D. Williams, 'Variability of brand price elasticities across retail stores: Ethnic, income, and brand determinants', *Journal of Retailing*, 00224359, Vol. 74, Issue 3, Fall 1998.

secure good retail distribution. As a result, they had suddenly become the dynamic force in the marketplace, jumping from 28% market share to 36% in just nine months. Marlboro, on the other hand, was losing share at a rate of half a percent each month.

Corrective action was obviously called for, and when it came it caused a good deal of excitement and consternation in the world of marketing. The reporting in the *Sunday Times* typifies the sense of melodrama which surrounds Marlboro's response:

> On April 2 1993, Philip Morris, the world's largest consumer-products group, took the biggest gamble of its life. It slashed the price in America of its top selling cigarette, Marlboro, by 20% – 40 cents – a pack.[6]

Marlboro's decision, subsequently described as a 'pricing earthquake', has been extensively analysed – so much that it is now known, somewhat fatefully, as 'Marlboro Friday'. To many, the price cut did indeed appear portentous, seeming to indicate the end of a golden age of branding. One of the world's strongest brands had been humbled by a few cheap, virtually unbranded products. Philip Morris's share price collapsed, losing 23% by the end of the day. This was followed by large drops for many other consumer goods companies. In the *Wall Street Journal*, Shapiro wrote:

> For makers of all consumer goods, Philip Morris' action is a milestone in marketing, the most dramatic evidence yet of a fundamental shift in consumer buying habits . . . More and more, consumers are by-passing household names for the cheaper, no-name products . . . This shows that even the biggest and strongest brands in the world are vulnerable.[7]

With the advantage of hindsight, this was in fact an astute strategic move for Philip Morris: the price cut effectively froze the unbranded sector, and caused considerable difficulties for Marlboro's branded competitors. Neither was 'Marlboro Friday' the Judgment Day for branding –

---

[6] *Sunday Times.*
[7] G. Shapiro, 'Cigarette burn: Price cut on Marlboro upsets rosy notions about tobacco profits', *Wall Street Journal*, 5 April 1993.

as Paul Feldwick was foremost in pointing out in his 1995 article 'Reports of the death of brands have been greatly exaggerated'.[8] Indeed, some commentators detect a real turning point for branding. Naomi Klein:

> On Marlboro Friday, a line was drawn in the sand between the lowly price slashers and the high-concept brand builders. The brand builders conquered and a new consensus was born: the products that will flourish in the future will be the ones presented not as 'commodities' but as concepts: the brand as experience, as lifestyle.[9]

STRONG BRANDS DON'T TAKE CONSUMERS FOR GRANTED

There is an important lesson to be drawn from the Marlboro story: don't take consumers for granted. An irresistible but flawed business logic compels companies to take as much profit as possible from a market, as quickly as possible. If prices can be pushed higher, push them higher. This logic drove Marlboro (and many others besides) to increase prices throughout the 1980s – but in doing so, they gradually lost the adherence of their mainstay consumers.

Strong brands may indeed have lower levels of price elasticity – but this often encourages them into complacency. In the 1960s, for example, Cadbury's were confident in the strength of their chocolate brands, and gradually increased the real price of its Dairy Milk chocolate bar by progressively reducing its thickness. Consumers happily continued buying the product – until competitor Rowntree exposed its devaluation by launching a new, thick and chunky brand, the 'Yorkie' bar.

At their peak, strong brands are prone to become victims of their own overbearing assumptions. Low price elasticity should perhaps be a cause for caution, rather than an occasion for hubris. All empires, they say, eventually over-extend themselves. Scott Bedbury, former marketing doyen at Nike, explains Marlboro's particular case of imperiousness:

---

[8] Paul Feldwick, 'Reports of the death of brands have been greatly exaggerated', *Marketing & Research Today*, 23(2), 1995.
[9] Naomi Klein, *No Logo*. Flamingo, 2001.

To me, the Marlboro Man had not fallen off his horse because the limitations of branding had finally revealed themselves. What sent him plummeting to earth, spurs pointing skyward, were two things: the product had lost any real differentiation in the marketplace from the equally blurred identities of a growing number of competitors, and its marketing strategy had become entirely predictable.[10]

A major benefit of a brand may be in supporting price – but to do this it should be built upon clear product differentiation, and certainly not by carrying on as if consumers are a bunch of hapless stooges.

VALUE CHECK

- Does your industry typically have high or low levels of price elasticity?

- Which brand in your industry has the lowest levels of price elasticity?

- If it's a competitor, what is it doing differently?

- If it isn't a competitor, can you be *absolutely* sure you aren't taking your customers for granted?

---

[10] Scott Bedbury (with Stephen Fenichell) *A New Brand World*. Penguin Books, 2003.

10

Strong Brands can Command a Premium

Source of Business Value: Brands can enable businesses to charge more for their products and services

IN CONVERSATION

Let's face it – for most people, spending money is one of life's great thrills. That's why luxury brands exist – to satisfy our craving for wanton, gratuitous spending. I think sometimes consumers *want* to pay more.

Mark Earls, Ogilvy & Mather

A premium brand means higher margins, which means you can create a kind of virtuous cycle. For us, higher margins mean more money to invest in delivering a quality customer experience, which further strengthens our brand's premium.

John Hayes, CMO, American Express

A strong brand may be able to follow a premium price strategy: setting the price above the category averages in order to give the brand an air of superior quality. This can be a source of real value to a business: by providing the consumers with a sense of reassurance about the quality of products and services, brands enable companies to increase their margins by raising their prices.

CONSUMERS SOMETIMES *WANT* TO PAY MORE

Economics students are told an apocryphal story about a shop clerk who mis-priced handkerchiefs at £15 instead of £1.50 – only to find that they all sold out. In many categories, people are not deterred by higher prices; to the contrary, a high price serves to reassure them about the quality of the product.

In fact, price may make a real difference to the consumer's experience of the product. To an extent, a consumer's satisfaction comes not just from the commodity itself, but also from the price paid for it: in the consumer's eyes, price is a significant part of the overall quality of the product.

This is particularly true for very visible brands which reflect the status (or aspirations) of the consumer. The idea of 'conspicuous consumption' was first raised in 1899 by the economist Thorstein Veblen, in his book *The Theory of the Leisure Class*. He paints an enthralling picture of life in the late nineteenth century:

> Conspicuous consumption of valuable goods is a means of rep-utability to the gentleman of leisure . . . . He becomes a connoisseur in creditable viands of various degrees of merit, in manly beverages and trinkets, in seemly apparel and architecture, in weapons, games, dancers, and the narcotics. This cultivation of aesthetic faculty requires time and application. . . .[1]

Veblen's gentlemen of leisure may belong to a different age, but the 'con-spicuous consumption of valuable goods' is bigger business than ever – at least, in much of the world. Sending signals about social standing remains a motivation behind many purchasing decisions, although it has since become encoded into a complex range of brands and prices.

---

[1] Thorstein Veblen, *The Theory of the Leisure Class*, New York, 1899; http://xroads. virginia.edu/%7EHYPER/VEBLEN/.

PREMIUM PRICING CAN DRIVE PREFERENCE

According to Veblen, conspicuous consumption can be seen most clearly in the 'manly beverages' – beer, spirits and wine. A well-known contemporary example of premium pricing comes from the Belgian brewers Interbrew, whose beer Stella Artois has become established throughout much of Europe as a high-quality lager – despite being thought of in its home country as a rather standard product.

For many years Stella Artois has promoted its 'Reassuringly Expensive' brand position, with premium pricing and using quality advertising to dramatize the sacrifices people make to drink the beer. As a result, the brand has dominated the premium position in many markets, in particular the UK. This is a tried-and-tested formula in many categories, but especially beverages: in 1967, for example, Johnny Walker Black Label ran a US campaign that declared 'At $9.45 it's expensive'.[2]

Intuitively, it makes sense that strong brands can support premium prices. Empirically, we can see evidence for this in Table 10.1, which compares the price index of five key U.K. beer brands with a measure of brand strength (bonding). As is the case in many categories, the brand with the greatest level of bonding – in this case Stella Artois – sustains the highest price index.

Table 10.1   Price index and bonding for premium UK beer brands

	Stella Artois	Budweiser	Guinness	Beck's	Kronenbourg
Price index	1.35	1.28	1.2	1.2	1.19
Bonding	18%	12%	5%	4%	3%

---

[2] B.P. Shapiro, 'The psychology of pricing', *Harvard Business Review*, July–August 1968.

CONSUMERS USE PRICE AS A GUIDE TO QUALITY

Nowhere does price become more integral to the experience of the product than in the world of wines – and nowhere is the objective assessment of quality so obscure. The ranking of Bordeaux wine, for example, is undertaken by a jury who must grade the wines according to some melodious criteria: '. . . the aromatic intensity of the wine, the finesse of the aromas, the complexity of the aromas . . . the firmness of the attack, the suppleness of the wine, the flatness, whether the wine is considered fat, the harmony between the components, the finish, etc. . . .'[3] It's no surprise that those with less elevated taste-buds – yet who still want to buy an acceptable wine – may let price be their guide.

Unfortunately, the relationship between the price and quality of a wine seems spurious at best. Many studies show that most people are unable to predict the price of a wine from a blind taste test. Even when a gathering of the world's most famous wine swillers was summoned to a blind test in 1995 by the Bordeaux-loving billionaire G. Getty, they could reach no convincing agreement.[4] As one of these world-leading quaffers confided to *The Economist* (he preferred to remain anonymous): 'Actually, these differences that everybody makes so much of are pretty tiny. My first rule of wine is that basically it all tastes the same.'[5]

PREMIUM PRICING WORKS BEST IN CERTAIN CATEGORIES

Price acts as a guide to quality in categories where big quality differences are suspected. If the quality of wine was more-or-less the same, then consumers would buy the cheapest; it's precisely because people think that there are big quality differences between wines that certain preferences develop for more expensive wines. It has long been the job of advertis-

---

[3] P. Combris, S. Lecocq and M. Visser, 'Estimation of a Hedonic price equation for Bordeaux wine: Does quality matter?'. *The Economic Journal*, 107 (March), 390–402.

[4] See footnote 3.

[5] 'The Price Puzzle', *The Economist*, 18/12/99.

ing to persuade us that big quality differences exist between brands, in order to justify prices. Certainly, consumers have been quick to accept that big quality differences exist in categories where the product appears more complex or technical – such as cars or electronic equipment.

In reality, the quality gap between products is falling in many categories. For example, when J.D. Power undertook a survey into standards in the global automotive industry, they reached the following conclusion: there's no such thing as a bad car. In this category, the brand transforms the customer's experience of the product: a BMW driver, for example, might enjoy the drive slightly less if the car was re-branded Hyundai. However, as different car manufacturers begin to approach similar levels of quality, the challenge for car brands will be to maintain their premium value.

MAINTAINING A PREMIUM CAN BE CHALLENGING

Even in categories such as electronics, where consumers have been ready to accept premium pricing, maintaining prices can be difficult. Sony, for example, have long dominated the premium electronics market, trading on a well-deserved reputation for innovation and design. However, this dominance has been challenged by competitors like Samsung and Sharp, who have re-tooled in order to close the quality gap. During the 1990s Sony experienced a slow, miserable slide into a low-margin commodity business: operating profits fell from 10% in 1991 to 1% in 2001.[6] Although Sony is acknowledged to be one of the strongest global brands, this alone will not help the company to sustain its margins in the face of changing market conditions. As Japan's analysts persist in pointing out, 'Sony needs a new business model'.[7]

---

[6] I. Kunii, C. Edwards and J. Greene, 'Can Sony regain the magic?', *Business Week*, 3.11.2002, issue 3773.
[7] T. Yamamoto, DM of Morgan Stanley Dean Witter Japan Ltd, quoted in Kunii *et al.* (see footnote 6).

THE PATH TO PREMIUM VALUE

Brand strength is not a passport to premium pricing, as the example of Sony demonstrates – but it is certainly a necessary prerequisite. When the conditions are right, price and brand can fall into a partnership, beguiling consumers into feeling good about paying more. Driving preference through a premium price strategy may sound like a dream come true – but many brands do successfully grow market share by charging more for their products or services.

It is more than a century since Thorstein Veblen described the important social role played by our consumption choices – and today we are still invited to purchase demonstrations of wealth and status (to varying degrees of subtlety). However, many people have become less concerned with showing off their money by paying premium prices. Increasingly, people seek to signal their values, and subtler qualities such as *authenticity* and *originality* move to the fore. Brands seeking the path to premium value in the future should remember this. As sociologist John Clammer observes: 'Shopping is not merely the acquisition of things, it is the buying of identity.'[8]

VALUE CHECK

- How do your customers perceive the quality of your products or services, compared to your competitors?

- How big is the perceived 'quality gap' in your category – i.e. the perceived differences in quality between brands?

- Which brand in your category commands the highest premium? How are they able to do this?

- What would happen to your customers' perceptions of quality if you increased your prices? What stops you doing this?

---

[8] John Clammer, quoted in D. Lewis and D. Bridger, *The Soul of the New Consumer*, Nicholas Brealey, 2000.

11

Strong Brands can Deal with Market Disruption

Source of Business Value: Brands sometimes help companies to maintain performance during times of uncertainty

IN CONVERSATION

We learned that, if your brand really means something, you stand a chance of overcoming market disruptions. At the end of the day, a company will only survive if it really believes in itself.

Steve Hayden, Ogilvy & Mather

Strong brands can sometimes show great resilience during times of change and upheaval. In many respects this seems self-evident: brands such as Lux, Levis, Cadbury, Ford and American Express have survived periods of massive disruption – both within their markets, and in the world at large. Some companies even use periods of disruption as opportunities to gain advantage. What's their secret?

WHEN BAD NEWS IS GOOD FOR BUSINESS

According to Bill Gates, bad news is good for business: 'You have to be consistently receptive to bad news, and then you have to act on it.'

According to Gates, the free-flow of bad news is crucial to his company's survival:

> Sometimes I think my most important job as CEO is to listen for bad news. If you don't act on it, your people will eventually stop bringing bad news to your attention. And that's the beginning of the end.[1]

Why is bad news so important? It's obviously good to have a balanced view of company performance – but there's a bigger picture: bad news may be an indication that the rules of the game are changing. For example, consumer preferences may be shifting, or competitive advantages may have been neutralized. The management consultants call this *market disruption*, defined by Bain & Company as 'a trend or event that leads to a shift of market power from established to emerging players'.[2]

COMMERCIAL CLOUT IS OFTEN MORE IMPORTANT

Strong brands often show great resilience in the face of market disruption. However, this is frequently a result of their commercial clout, rather than the strength of the brand. When faced with a revolution in their marketplace, big brands may seek to contain the damage by locking-in customers. For example, United and American did much to blunt the attack from the US low-cost airlines through their frequent-flier incentive programs.[3] In the UK, British Airways tried to spend their way out of the problem by founding their own upstart airline, Go.

Big players may even move to neutralize market disruptions through the courts. For example, when the music industry's dominant business model was threatened by the file-sharing revolutionaries Napster, the major labels responded by shutting down the challenger through legal

---

[1] Bill Gates, *Business @ The Speed of Thought*. Penguin Books, 2000.
[2] Bain & Company website, www.bain.com.
[3] Richard D'Aveni, 'The Empire Strikes Back', *Harvard Business Review*, November 2002.

action. However, internet file-sharing still threatens to overturn existing market structures.

STRONG BRANDS MAY EVEN BE A HINDRANCE IN TIMES OF CHANGE

Attempts to defend the status quo against disruption are seldom successful in the long term, but such defence is a common impulse: faced with a major market disruption, most big brands retreat into their conventional precepts. As Accenture chairman Vernon Ellis puts its: 'History suggests that the response to great shocks is often to take a highly conservative and defensive approach, cutting costs and focusing on core markets.' Such a response is understandable, according to Ellis, but it means that opportunities are overlooked:

> For those businesses that are willing and able to act decisively, uncertainty and dislocation can provide a real impetus for greater innovation, as they look for new solutions to cope with changed conditions.[4]

Are strong brands better at turning disruptions into opportunities? We believe that, in many cases, they may be a hindrance in times of change. Like a big ship, a strong brand may weather the storm, but is not quick to manoeuvre. The very factors from which a brand derives its strength – the apparatus of the brand, together with relevant consumer perceptions – may act as a straitjacket to limit change.

TURNING DISRUPTIONS INTO OPPORTUNITIES

Most big brands have well-established presumptions about the market. These shared presumptions are essential to the smooth running of any

---

[4] Vernon Ellis, *Business in a Fragile World*, www.accenture.com.

large, complex organization – but when a market disruption occurs, they can make it difficult to see what's really going on. Too often, people's perceptions of the situation are limited by subtle doctrines: *the way things work* and *the way we do things.*

A striking account of breaking through such presumptions comes from Royal Dutch/Shell, which was the only major oil company prepared for the oil price shock that followed the 1973 Yom Kippur war. The company's executives responded quickly because they were prepared for the possibility of disruption – Shell's head of strategy, Pierre Wack, had worked with them on a series of scenarios about the future.

But Wack wasn't trying to *forecast* the future, just *prepare* for it. When he first published his approach – later known as 'scenario planning' – the article was titled 'The gentle art of re-perceiving'.[5] As Pierre's successor at Shell, Peter Schwartz, put it, 'Pierre was not interested in predicting the future. His goal was the liberation of people's insights.'[6]

THINKING LIKE A CHALLENGER BRAND

Because of their size, strong brands may be able to absorb market shocks – but they are frequently slow to recognize them, and rarely approach them as opportunities. On the other hand, small challenger brands are quicker to respond to market shocks, and more effective at disrupting the status quo. Much of this, we believe, is cultural: challenger brands do not have such well-entrenched narratives about how the world works, and find it easier to re-perceive their markets.

In times of disruption, people working for big brands need to adopt more of a challenger mentality – to resist the defensive impulse, and look for new opportunities. However, people are often afraid to challenge the mythologies that surround their brand. As Intel Corporation co-founder Andrew Grove warns: 'Unless you deal with this fear, unless you live this

---

[5] Pierre Wack, 'Scenarios: the gentle art of re-perceiving', Havard Business School working paper, 1984.
[6] Peter Schwartz, *The Art of the Long View*, John Wiley & Sons, 1991.

fear, you will never hear from those helpful Cassandras and you are going to be late in responding."[7]

VALUE CHECK

- How good are you are listening to bad news?

- List two assumptions about your business which may be wrong. What would you do if they *were* wrong?

- List two possible major disruptions to your market. How would you respond to each?

- Look at your responses to the last question. Are they defensive or opportunistic?

---

[7] Andrew Grove, speech to the Academy of Management Executives 1999.

12

Strong Brands have more Loyalty

Source of Business Value: Brands can lead to higher levels of repeat purchase among consumers

IN CONVERSATION

What makes every strong brand strong is a core of loyal, high-value category buyers, who typically account for more than half of brand sales.

Garth Hallberg, author of *All Consumers Are Not Created Equal*

People are herd animals. We see this over and over – consumers may settle on a brand for a while, and then something changes, some trigger happens, and suddenly the whole herd takes off and settles somewhere else, with some other brand. Sure, strong brands have more loyal customers – but the real trick is to understand the triggers, to get to know how the herd behaves.

Mark Earls, Ogilvy & Mather

We talk about strong brands having loyal customers, but people aren't stupid and this loyalty isn't blind. If their needs change or something better comes along – and their brand does nothing to respond – they will be gone.

Jon Steel, WPP

Customer loyalty has become something of a holy grail in marketing, based upon a belief that building a strong brand can deliver higher levels of repeat purchase. In order to understand this belief, we briefly examine its origins.

FROM CUSTOMER SATISFACTION TO EMOTIONAL LOYALTY

Until the 1980s, most people thought that the key to maintaining loyalty was customer satisfaction. This was questioned in a landmark book by W. Edwards Deming, who argued that a customer who is satisfied today may have a different set of needs tomorrow.[1] Since then, much work has been done to prove that satisfaction scores alone do not predict how customers will actually behave. Of course, satisfaction is necessary to keep customers loyal – but it's not always enough: studies of many brands, including British Airways, American Express and IBM, demonstrated that satisfied customers were often disloyal.[2]

A new perspective quickly emerged. Satisfaction scores, it was said, measured the rational, functional aspects of a customer's experience; they were purely backward looking, and didn't capture the customer's emotions about the brand. Organizations such as Gallup undertook extensive research to establish the importance of measuring what they called the *emotional dynamic*, arguing that 'people stay faithful to brands that earn both their rational trust and their deeply held affection'.[3]

These arguments were pulled together by Frederick F. Reichheld in his book *The Loyalty Effect*, published in 1996.[4] Reichheld's research showed that the cost of acquiring new customers was five times the cost of servicing existing ones – with the clear implication that building loyalty should be a strategic priority for any brand.

---

[1] W. Edwards Deming, *Out of the Crisis*, MIT Press, 2000.
[2] See, for example, T.O. Jones and W. Earl Sasser, Jr, 'Why satisfied customers defect', *Harvard Business Review*, Nov.–Dec. 1995.
[3] Alec Applebaum, *The constant customer*, Gallup Management Journal, 17 June 2001.
[4] Frederick F. Reichheld, *The Loyalty Effect*, Harvard Business School Press, 1996.

A BRAND'S LOYALTY IS CORRELATED TO ITS STRENGTH

The emphasis on loyalty was further strengthened by the publication of Garth Hallberg's book *All Consumers Are Not Created Equal*, which showed that a small percentage of consumers were responsible for the majority of a brand's sales.[5] According to Hallberg, each brand has a core of loyal, high-value customers – these are the engine of the brand's financial value.

Thus, building loyalty has become enshrined as a key marketing objective for all companies: strong brands are expected to deliver plenty of loyal, highly valuable customers. One common method of estimating levels of loyalty is *share of requirements* (SOR) – which measures a brand's sales volume as a share of the total category volume. For example, if I purchase in a product category 10 times in one year, and I purchase the same brand 6 times, that brand's share of my requirement is 60%. Averaging share of requirement across the brand's customer base gives its SOR score – a useful indication of levels of loyalty.

The conventional wisdom holds that building a strong brand can help build SOR – and this pattern can be seen across many markets. Using WPP's *Brandz*™ data, we measured correlations between brand strength and SOR, for seven randomly selected markets and categories. To estimate brand strength, we used 'bonding' scores, which measure consumers' emotional attachment to a brand. The results in Table 12.1 show that correlations tend to be high.

IS LOYALTY DRIVEN BY A BRAND'S STRENGTH, OR ITS SIZE?

There is clearly a correlation between a brand's strength and its SOR – and numerous studies have been carried out to support this. However, this doesn't necessarily prove that brand strength *causes* loyalty. Ehrenberg,

---

[5] Garth Hallberg, *All Consumers Are Not Created Equal*, John Wiley & Sons, 1995.

Table 12.1   Correlation between brand strength (bonding) and loyalty (share of requirement)

Category	Country	Correlation
Airlines	USA	0.927
Beers	UK	0.902
Mineral water	France	0.773
Midsize cars	Germany	0.882
Hair care	Japan	0.903
Banking	Mexico	0.967
Newspapers	Canada	0.984

Table 12.2   Annual buying rates for fabric conditioners

Brands (by market share)	% Buying in year	Average purchase rate
Downy	48	3.6
Snuggle	34	3.1
Bounce	18	1.7
Cling	8	2.0
Arm & Hammer	5	2.1

for example, believes that it isn't the brand's *strength* that causes loyalty, but its *size*: 'Marketing inputs cannot increase loyalty much or for long unless the brand's penetration [number of buyers] is increased.'[6]

Ehrenberg and his associates have shown repeatedly that loyalty – a brand's share of requirements – can be predicted from penetration. Table 12.2 shows a typical case where SOR is greater for brands with higher penetration. Similar results have been found for market share (the share of total category spend commanded by a brand).[7]

---

[6] A. Ehrenberg and G. Goodhardt, 'Double jeopardy revisited, again', *Marketing Research*, Spring 2001.

[7] A. Ehrenberg and J. Scriven, 'Added values or propensities to buy', *JOAB Report 1*, South Bank Business School, London.

SMALL BRANDS SUFFER FROM 'DOUBLE JEOPARDY'

This effect has become known as 'double jeopardy', referring to the plight of smaller brands: 'The small brand is punished twice for being small: It has fewer buyers, and these few buyers are somewhat less loyal.'[8]

This situation has a direct parallel in the field of ecology. Successful species, such as the *brown rat* or *starling*, tend to be broadly distributed and live in high-density populations. In fact, research shows that more widely distributed species also tend to occur at higher local densities.[9] This means that, like Ehrenberg's smaller brands, rarer species face a double jeopardy: if they are distributed across a narrow geographical range, they are also likely to live in smaller populations – and hence face a greater risk of extinction. To escape double jeopardy, small species must either challenge the dominance of larger ones, or find an ecological niche – and the same approach applies to small brands.

Some small species live at high densities in a narrow ecological niche – such as the *mud skipper* of Florida, which is found only in the mangrove swamps. These species may sustain their populations, but are always more vulnerable to sudden changes in their environment. Of course, the term *niche* has been borrowed by marketers in this sense, and Ehrenberg suggests that it may be possible for some niche brands to exist – those that are bought relatively often by a relatively small group of people.

LEVELS OF LOYALTY ARE DECLINING

People are becoming less and less loyal to the brands they buy. Consumer surveys reveal falling levels of loyalty over an extended period – see, for example, Figure 12.1. A mixture of factors contribute to this decline:

- Consumers have become increasingly confident and aware of their options, and as a result are more likely to view every transaction on its merits.

---

[8] See footnote 6.
[9] K. Gaston, 'Rarity as double jeopardy', *Nature*, Vol. 394, July 1998.

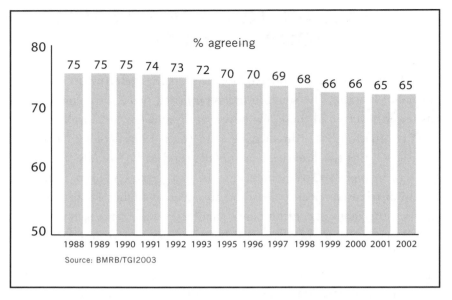

Figure 12.1 *Declining levels of consumer loyalty: % agreeing with the statement 'When I find a brand I like, I tend to stick with it'.*

- It has become increasingly easy to compare rival offers, particularly since the arrival of the internet, and this enables consumers to go for the best deal each time.
- For many consumers, loyalty cards have encouraged a discount mentality to shopping. As Mike Watkins from AC Nielsen comments, 'Discount shoppers in the UK are the most promiscuous of all shopper types'.[10]
- Increasingly, people seek variety and like to try new brands and products; boredom thresholds have fallen and consumers like to break out of same-old routines – and this has had a negative impact on loyalty.

DOES CUSTOMER LOYALTY REALLY EXIST?

Some people are beginning to question whether the entire concept of customer loyalty is a marketing conceit. Certainly, the idea often seems

---

[10] Quoted in David Lewis *et al.*, *The Soul of The New Consumer*, Nicholas Brealey, 2000.

bizarre to consumers themselves – as one research respondent responded, 'it's not necessarily being loyal to the product that is at issue, but being loyal to myself'.[11] In other words, the consumers' first priority is to satisfy themselves, and the idea of being loyal to a brand is largely irrelevant to them. When someone asked Jeff Bezos – CEO of Amazon.com – whether his customers were loyal, he replied: 'Absolutely! 100%. Right 'till the moment someone else comes along and offers a better service.'[12]

THE PATH TO LOYALTY

In plain English, *loyalty* implies some form of attachment or allegiance. Although this seems like an overstatement of the relationship between brand and consumer, we believe that some form of emotional loyalty can exist. It's a rare thing – but even today's knowledgeable consumers can bond to a brand. We discuss drivers of bonding more fully in Part 5. There are, broadly speaking, two ways to engender loyalty.

- *Stand for something*
  Why does a brand such as Apple inspire a devoted core of profitable customers? What excites people about Apple is the *purpose* of the company: enthusiasts really do feel that the company is committed to developing technology to unleash the creativity inside all of us. If customers can embrace the company's sense of purpose, they are more likely to form emotional bonds. This applies to staff also – which is essential to ensuring that the company delivers against the customer's expectations.

- *Over-deliver – consistently*
  Authentic emotional loyalty is generated when a company consistently over-delivers against the consumer's best expectations. For example, American Express provides occasional unexpected treats to card

---

[11] Susan Fournier, 'Consumers and their brands: Developing relationship theory in consumer research', *Journal of Consumer Research*, 24 (March), 343–373, 1998.

[12] Quoted in Drayton Bird, 'Don't worry about loyalty, small brands simply need to sell more', *Marketing (UK)*, 11/2002.

members – such as a recent 10% reduction for card members shopping in the Harrod's January sale. American Express customers are delighted by occasional surprises such as this; not only are they more likely to remain with the brand, but they are also more likely to recommend it to others.

VALUE CHECK

Put yourself in the shoes of a competitor, intent on poaching your brand's consumers. How would a competitor set about doing this? What would you do to defend against their actions?

What do you think your brand stands for, in the eyes of consumers?

List three simple, cost effective things you could do to surpass your customers' expectations.

Can you identify your most important customers?

13

Strong Brands are a Store of Trust

Source of Business Value: Brands can engender trust amongst consumers – leading to more sales and higher prices.

IN CONVERSATION

Brands are a storehouse of trust.

Niall FitzGerald, Unilever

We live in a world where *trust* has become a scare resource – yet, at the same time, people must deal with more uncertainty and make more choices than ever before. I think there's a role here for brands to play.

Will Galgey, The Henley Centre

The trust of our customers is our greatest asset. Wherever they are, our customers know what American Express stands for – and at the end of the day, I think that's at the heart of our business.

John Hayes, CMO, American Express

It was Unilever's chairman, Niall FitzGerald, who described the brand as 'a storehouse of trust'. Speaking to *The Economist*, he argued that the role of brands has become more important, not less: '[the brand] matters more

Figure 13.1 *People are more likely to trust 'their' brands (source:* Henley World, *2003)*

and more as choices multiply. People want to simplify their lives.'[1] This is a source of value for businesses: if people trust your brand they are more likely to buy it, and more likely to pay more for it.

There is clearly a relationship between consumers' feelings of trust towards a brand and their behaviour. A Henley Centre study into trust demonstrated that for banks, newspapers and political parties, people are substantially more likely to trust 'their' brand (see Figure 13.1).

BRANDS ARE A CONSUMER'S GUARANTEE OF QUALITY

Brands began as a straightforward guarantee of quality and consistency – and for this, naturally, consumers were prepared to pay a premium. As Jeremy Bullmore puts it, 'brands were the first piece of consumer protection – you knew where to go when you had a complaint'.[2] History shows

---

[1] Jeremy Bullmore, quoted in 'Who's wearing the trousers?', *The Economist*, 6 September 2001.
[2] See footnote 1.

that unbranded production leads to a deterioration in quality: in the former Soviet Union, central planners were forced to introduce 'production marks' to prevent manufacturers from cutting corners.[3]

Trust explains the premium prices achieved by brands such as American Express and IBM: people are prepared to pay more because they are sure that they'll get a certain level of quality. An interesting illustration comes from the online auctioneer eBay, which encourages buyers to rate the service they receive from sellers. Researchers have investigated the prices that an established eBay seller achieves, compared with the same products offered by an unrated seller. After 200 transactions, the researchers found that the established seller was able to charge 7.6% more.[4]

BRANDS HELP CONSUMERS' TO REDUCE RISK

Economists writing about trust often link it to *risk* – for example, 'trust involves action in which there is vulnerability or a risk of adverse consequences'.[5] Thus it makes sense to talk of trusting Southwest Airlines, Nurofen or Visa, since the failure of these brands to deliver on their promises may be painful. Similarly, when the product may be technical or complex – such as PCs, or audio equipment – trust may also be important, since people want to offset the risk that the product may be prone to failure.

In a sense, this works in the same way that we might pay a premium to an insurance company, to offset a range of other risks. In the eBay example, people are paying a premium to offset the risk that they may get ripped off. It seems that people will pay more for brands if the risk of disappointment is perceived to be lower. Brands, then, help consumers to manage the risks involved with their various transactions: perceived risk is lower from brands that are tried and familiar ('it worked last time, why change?').

---

[3] See footnote 1.
[4] A. Powell, 'Putting a dollar value on a good name', *Harvard University Gazette*; http://www.news.harvard.edu/gazette/2003/02.27/17-ebay.html
[5] M. Korczynski, 'The political economy of trust', in *Journal of Management Studies*, January 2000.

TRUST HAS BECOME A SCARCE RESOURCE

Many of our ideas about branding were formed in the 1950s and 1960s. Consumers in this period had grown up with post-war shortages, when people would gratefully buy whatever they could access. This, together with a diet of paternalistic public-sector broadcasting, produced a generation of compliant consumers. However, people have become increasingly reluctant to place their trust in brands – they are increasingly questioning and suspicious. Why is this?

Academics such as Robert Putnam and Francis Fukuyama attribute the fall in levels of trust to diminishing *social capital*: 'The decline in a wide range of social structures like neighborhoods, churches, unions, clubs, and charities; and the general sense among Americans of a lack of shared values and community with those around them'.[6] As many of the world's economies become increasingly low-trust societies, so a new generation of consumer has emerged – more likely to check labels, compare prices and scrutinize propositions. In this environment, a high-trust brand is a real competitive advantage.

THE IMPORTANCE OF TRUST DEPENDS UPON THE CATEGORY

Surveys about trust seem to show high levels of trust for brands like Nokia, IBM and Colgate.[7] But when people say 'I trust Nokia', what do they really mean? A clue lies in the fact that surveys about trust always concentrate on certain categories, such as airlines, pain relief and credit cards. Clearly, it would be slightly bizarre to claim 'I trust Sprite', and people might wonder what you meant if you were to tell them 'I trust Johnny Walker'.

It seems that trust is in some way linked to function – as Mark Earls pointed out, bemoaning a UK survey which purported to show that people trust Tesco's supermarket more than they trust the police: 'We trust super-

---

[6] F. Fukuyama, *Trust: the Social Virtues of the Creation of Prosperity*, The Free Press, 1995.
[7] Reader's Digest Trusted Brands Survey, 2003.

markets to be good supermarkets, rather than enforce law and order. . . .'[8]
When thinking about trust in relation to brands, it's important to be clear
about the role and importance of trust: What is the brand being trusted
to do?

TRUST IS BORN OUT OF FAMILIARITY

People are more likely to trust the things they know. This leads to some
slightly odd results: research by MORI in the UK shows that levels of
trust for individual MPs are higher than those for parliament – even
though parliament consists exclusively of MPs. Similarly, more people
trust local councillors than local councils.[9] Individual persons seem more
familiar – and more trustworthy – than distant institutions.

The Henley Centre found that, in six markets studied, people are consistently more likely to trust companies from their own country than
multinationals (see Figure 13.2). Whereas familiarity may engender trust,

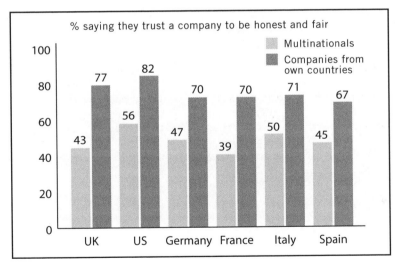

Figure 13.2 *People are more likely to trust local companies (source:*
Henley World, 2003)

[8] Mark Earls, 'Learning to live without the brand', in M. Earls and M. Baskin (eds), *Brand
New Brand Thinking*, Kogan Page, 2002.
[9] MORI, *Exploring Trust in Public Institutions*. Report for the Audit Commission.

foreignness may engender some suspicion. A sense of familiarity seems an important part of building trust.

THE PATH TO TRUST

Strictly speaking, *trust* is a term taken from the domain of human relationships. Consumers in focus groups find it easy to articulate their feelings using this kind of language, and it makes intuitive sense to marketers. However, there is no easy seven-step guide to building trust with consumers: real trust comes from having a clear brand strategy and delivering upon it consistently over time. As Niall FitzGerald puts it:

> Trust . . . can't be built in a one-off spate of advertising. Trust is built over the long term, on the basis not of communication but of action. And then again, trust, once established, can be lost in an instant – one ill-judged remark and it's gone forever.[10]

VALUE CHECK

- What do you want people to trust you to *do?*

- Which kinds of people currently trust you the most?

- Which brand is the most trusted brand in your category?

- If it isn't you – what do they have that you don't (apart from market share!)

- If it is you – list the top three things that could jeopardize this trust?

---

[10] Niall FitzGerald, Chairman, Unilever, Address to the Advertising Association, May 2001.

14

Strong Brands can Stimulate Innovation

Source of Business Value: Brands can help to create new ideas for products and services.

IN CONVERSATION

A strong brand is like a north star for a company's research and development efforts – it guides the imagination of the organization in commercially useful directions.

Steve Hayden, Ogilvy & Mather

Great brands have a licence to thrill. Consumers trust them, expect more from them and part of that expectation is that they will innovate successfully.

Marie-Louise Neil, Group Strategic Development Director, Research International

Innovation can be glamorous and seductive. But in order to be successful, it should take place with strong, effective branding.

Irwin Gotlieb, CEO, Group M

It's the holy grail of business: finding that category-busting new product or revolutionary new service that will blow away the competition. A number of studies have shown the link between effective research and development (R&D) and business performance measures such as sales growth, share prices and shareholder returns. A UK government study

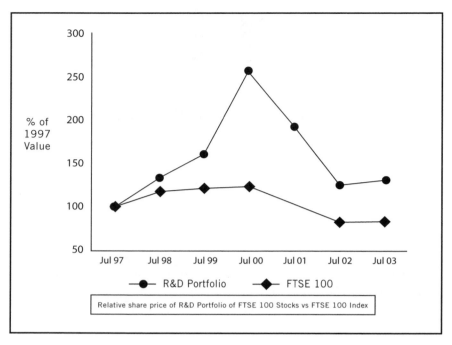

Figure 14.1 *Companies with strong R&D operations out-perform the average (source: R&D Scoreboard by the UK Department of Trade & Industry)*

into companies with high-quality R&D operations demonstrated that these companies command a premium share price (see Figure 14.1).

Innovation is the ultimate source of business value. In fact, the importance of innovation is such that it seems self-evident. We've identified several perspectives from which innovation adds value to a business:

- It creates new products and services – and thus new markets.
- It creates enhancements to existing products and services – and thus a source of differentiation and competitive advantage.
- It can be the only path to business growth when existing markets are saturated.
- It can stimulate consumer demand by creating novelty and excitement – this supporting volume and/or value.

Given the importance of innovation to business, a steady slurry of books and articles are published on the subject. Type the word 'innovation' into

Google and you'll get an endless list of business pap. But the simple truth is that no watertight process exists that can guarantee success – if there were, the failure rate for new products would be considerably lower. Currently, as many as 90% of new products fail.[1] Clearly, innovation is not easy – at least, not for most people.

STRONG BRANDS GIVE PURPOSE TO INNOVATION

Innovation has been promoted as the core factor of business success – innovate or die, we are told. The management gurus queue up to deliver the same sermon: innovation is the soul of entrepreneurship, it's the new imperative. We might be forgiven for thinking that companies can boost profits by simply fostering creativity.

But innovation for its own sake doesn't get us very far. Innovation can sometimes be pointless – and when it is, it's unlikely to lead to business success. For an innovation to be successful, it must be embraced by the company, by its employees, and, of course, by consumers. Strong brands can play a role here: a clearly understood brand can symbolize the aspirations of the company – and thus provide direction to a company's R&D activities.

Apple – everyone's favourite example of an innovative company – has a clearly understood brand with a clear purpose: developing technologies that allow people to play around with images, videos and music. Everybody understands that Apple stands for excellence in design and innovation in technology. Apple's brand is clearly understood – and much loved – by employees and customers alike.

This gives Apple a crucial advantage: people working on new products have a deeply held understanding of why customers love Apple. They know what people expect from the company – and even what they might not expect, but would love anyway. In other words, the strength of Apple's brand gives the company an in-built market orientation. This permeates the company, giving a sense of purpose to the company's innovation activities.

---

[1] From the Market Research Society, www.marketresearch.org.uk

BRANDS PROVIDE IN-BUILT MARKET ORIENTATION

Market orientation – as opposed to *product* orientation – is obviously a key component of success. This is sometimes taken a little too far. Often, the route to innovation is a laborious haul through reams of quantitative research and hours of focus groups. The purveyors of such approaches may make incremental improvements on existing products, but rarely make any breakthroughs. As Stephen King memorably commented, 'They're hoping for a nice, neat, rank-ordered list of motivations so that the top half-dozen can be stuffed directly into products and advertising.'[2]

A strong brand can perhaps provide a better approach to market orientation, encapsulating a deep-rooted understanding of consumers and a well-developed stance towards them. Snapple and Ben & Jerry's both innovate constantly, and their efforts are all in the spirit of their brand. Dove's impressive range of brand extensions all flow from a consistent and well-understood brand position. Of course, there is a role for research to stimulate innovation; but not to lead it: as Henry Ford is said to have commented: 'If I'd asked consumers what they wanted I would have invented a faster horse.'

INNOVATING THE BUSINESS MODEL

Henry Ford didn't in fact invent the automobile – but he did invent the mass-production process that revolutionized manufacturing. Sometimes, innovations such as this are the most powerful of all. Compare, for example, Apple and Dell. Despite their second-to-none record of innovation, Apple has consistently been squeezed out of the markets they have invented. Converting innovation into cash has not been easy for the company: in 2003 – the year in which its iTunes was applauded by *Time* magazine as *The Coolest Invention of the Year* – Apple's operating profit slumped to a meager 0.4% – down from 20% in 1981.

---

[2] Stephen King speech to MRS Conference, 1983.

Unlike Apple, Dell hasn't innovated the product, but the business model. At no point has Dell done anything to make PCs faster, smaller, more powerful, or better-looking. Dell's great innovation has been in distribution – enabling it to deliver a wider range of products at a lower cost to a broader audience. As a result, Dell now sells more units than Apple.

Some companies, however, are able to excel at both product and business innovation – and especially service companies. American Express, for example, runs state-of-the-art customer service operations: this is an integral part of the service offering to customers, as well as an important component in the company's business model. By providing a first-rate service, American Express is able to maintain the prestige status of its brand, and thus support premium charges.

INNOVATIONS CAN BE ACCIDENTAL

Some ideas are accidental, the unintended consequences of solving a different problem. Pringles began life as somebody's idea for using up by-product potato paste, and became a market-leader brand in its own right. Of course, pizza, gazpacho and shepherd's pie were all originally ways for poorer families to use up leftovers, and have since become staples of many diets.

The telephone was another accidental idea. Its inventor, Alexander Graham Bell, did not set out to revolutionize long-distance communication: he was interested in educating the deaf, and developing a hearing aid for his deaf wife. When he filed the patent for a telephony device in 1871, some of his less far-sighted associates asked, 'And what would become of errand boys?'

INNOVATIONS CAN BE DISRUPTIVE

Some innovations have significant impacts on their marketplace. Those who are invested in the status quo may find their judgement obscured: Lee De Forest, pioneer of radio broadcasting, didn't think that television was such a hot idea: 'While theoretically and technically television may be feasible, commercially and financially I consider it an impossibility, a development of which we need waste little time dreaming.'

Certainly, evidence suggests that it's harder for larger companies to launch radical innovations because they may cannibalize existing products or services. As a result – and despite formidable R&D budgets – big companies struggle to push through an idea that may shake up the market. As Dr Susan Baker of Cranfield School of Management observes, 'Too often they begin the process wanting the big radical idea and end up with something very incremental.'[3]

Disruptive innovations are often the ammunition of hungry challenger brands. When online DVD lender NetFlix.com announced at the close of 2003 that it had nearly 1 300 000 subscribers – up 71% year-on-year – it was clear that their innovative video rental model had changed the category forever. Established players such as Blockbusters must find a way to respond or face a declining share of the market.

FORTUNE FAVOURS THE PREPARED MIND

We began by saying that there is no formula for innovation. There's no A-B-C process that is guaranteed to deliver a successful new product or service. But neither is innovation a matter of divine inspiration, something that involuntarily comes upon creative types (as Mark Earls puts it, 'like artistic gastro-enteritis').

'Eureka' moments are much misunderstood. Archimedes' discovery wasn't an unexpected bolt from the blue. When he stepped into his bath and suddenly realized that the displacement of water could be used to measure the volume of solids, he had been worrying about the problem for days. The story is illuminating: the tyrant of Syracuse had demanded that he find out if his crown was pure gold or not. Archimedes knew how much pure gold should weigh per pint – so the only method he could think of was to melt the crown, pour it into a pint and weigh it. Of course, melting the king's ornate headpiece wasn't really an option. If only there was another way to measure the volume of an object . . .

---

[3] Quoted in 'Where have all the ideas gone?', *Brand Strategy*, November 2003.

And so it was that Archimedes – preoccupied with ideas about weight and volume – absent-mindedly stepped into his daily bath, and solved the problem.[4] In a sense, he was *ready* for the idea: 'fortune favours the prepared mind', as Louis Pasteur famously said. There may be no formula for innovation, but new ideas are more likely to come to prepared minds. Strong brands, we believe, can play a role here.

A strong brand should embody the aspirations of the organization. It should align the efforts of the people inside the company with the tastes, preferences and needs of consumers. If employees have this frame of reference, they are simply more likely to see new and appropriate opportunities. A strong brand provides a sense of purpose to an organization – if you like, a sense of the future. Without this sense, it's harder to recognize opportunities, and innovation becomes impossible. As Arie de Geus writes:

> We will not perceive a signal from the outside world unless it is relevant to an option for the future that we have already worked out in our imaginations. The more 'memories of the future' we develop, the more open and receptive we will be to signals from the outside world.[5]

VALUE CHECK

- Is your business market-oriented or product-oriented? (Try to prove the opposite of your answer.)

- Where is innovation likely to occur in your business – e.g. in product development? In the business model? In communications? In distribution?

- Are your chances of successful innovation better or worse than your competitors? (Explain the difference.)

---

[4] This story is much better told in Arthur Koestler, *The Act of Creation* (Macmillan, 1970). Thanks to Jeremy Bullmore for the recommendation.
[5] Quoted in M. Earls and M. Baskin (eds), *Brand New Brand Thinking*, Kogan Page, 2002.

- Imagine how a successful innovation might change your business
  – e.g. in terms of differentiation from competitors, stimulating consumer excitement, disrupting the status quo, etc. (Write some
  headlines for different scenarios.)

PART III
Strategic Brand Planning

Part II reviewed the ways that a brand can contribute value to a business. This section examines the major strategic challenges that a brand may face – starting with the very basics: defining the market. How a business chooses to define its market is a critical (and often neglected) strategic decision, and we examine the issues involved.

There are a number of core challenges that a brand can expect to face over the course of time – this is the heart of strategic brand planning. We introduce them briefly below then describe the characteristics of each type of challenge in detail.

- *Launch* – introducing a brand to a market for the first time. This may be a new brand entering a well-defined market, or a completely new type of product. We discuss this in Chapter 17.
- *Challenge* – displacing dominant brands in the market. The market leaders often have the advantage of a consolidated position, and dislodging them often requires particularly ingenious planning. We discuss this in Chapter 18.
- *Maintain* – defending a market position. Strong brands need to stay strong by the use of such strategies as creating barriers to entry, locking in existing customers, or extending the brand into new areas. We discuss this in Chapter 19.
- *Revitalize* – bringing fresh life to an existing brand. Brands inevitably lose their shine from time to time, and strategies such as relaunch and repositioning may refresh them. We discuss this in Chapter 20.
- *Re-brand* – change the branding for a product, service, or company. We look at situations when this may be necessary, and examine approaches for successful re-branding. This is discussed in Chapter 21.

- *Acquire* – integrate an acquired brand into a portfolio. There are a number of possible pitfalls when taking on acquired brands and we look at some of these and learn from some high profile mistakes. We discuss this in Chapter 22.

15

Defining the Market

THE MARKET DEFINITION CYCLE

Two questions must be answered in order to define the market. Firstly, who are our customers? Secondly, what are we selling? Obviously these questions cannot be answered in isolation from each other. Often, a business begins with a clearly defined product or service offering, and then seeks to find the most profitable customers to sell it to. Alternatively, a business might begin with access to a customer base, and seeks to uncover demand for new products or services. Usually, defining a market involves a cycle between these two questions – *what?* and *who?* – as shown in Figure 15.1.

A full answer to the question *'Who are our customers?'* must contain both an attitudinal and demographic description of them, as well as some idea of time-scales. It can also be clarifying to describe who is *not* being targeted. An answer to the *'What are we selling?'* question must describe the proposed products or services, price structures and distribution – as well as outlining how the products or services will compete against rival offerings.

DEFINING THE MARKET IS A KEY STRATEGIC TASK

It should be clear that the task of defining the market is at the core of the business: a bold, insightful definition can be the difference

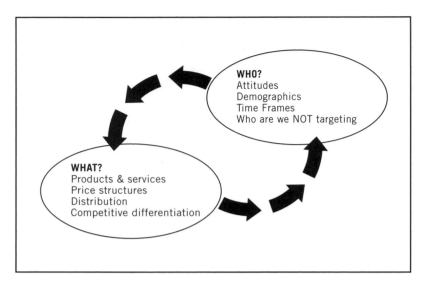

Figure 15.1   *Market definition cycle*

between success and failure. The car industry provides a classic example of this.

When Henry Ford pioneered mass production, he had a very clear idea of who his potential customers were: everyone. He also had a very clear idea of what he was selling: the *Model T* – a uniform product that conformed to the company's famous dictum: any colour, as long as it's black. In the 1920s, Ford commanded 60% of the American market with one model. The formula for success was simple: deliver a standardized product to a mass market that wanted the lowest possible prices.

For many years, competition to Ford was weak. General Motors was Number 2, struggling to hold onto a 12% market share – with eight different models. GM was on the brink of collapse when Alfred P. Sloan Jr became chief executive in 1921. He turned the company around by re-asking the question: What is our market? Sloan defined the market around several very stable income groups, and the company developed distinct brands to target each one. The result shows clearly why defining the market is a key strategic issue: within five years GM had the dominant market share – and a lasting legacy of classic brands, including Chevrolet, Buick and Cadillac.

The GM story holds one further lesson: customers change over time, and so must market definitions. GM's market definition was successful for many years, and it became engrained as a cultural truth within the company. However, in the 1970s customers started to behave differently. Income ceased to be the main factor influencing buying decisions. The old, stable income groups around which GM had structured its brands began to fragment, and fluid 'lifestyle' groups began to form. The company held on to the old market definitions, and so began a long decline in market share. In 1972 it was the fourth largest company in the world, and by 1992 it was the fortieth.

MARKET DEFINITION CAN REQUIRE TOUGH DECISIONS

The GM story shows what can be achieved through a strong, insightful definition of the market – and also demonstrates the risks of failing to keep this definition fresh and up-to-date. Defining the market often demands taking some tough decisions – particularly when answering the questions of *'what?'* and *'who?'* involves drawing some firm boundaries. Two examples demonstrate this:

- *Tough decisions: who are our customers?*
  In 1989 the Danish bank Lan & Spar was in financial trouble, and decided to take a fresh look at the question *'Who are our customers?'* Having decided to focus on white-collar workers, the bank wrote to all of its corporate customers (who accounted for some 25% of its deposits) and asked them to leave the bank. Culling your customer base may not seem the obvious solution for a struggling bank – but it enabled the business to focus its efforts behind a clear brand position. As a result, within three years the bank became Denmark's most profitable. By 1997 it had broken into Denmark's top 10 banks – from its 1989 position of 42.[1] Defining the market often involves being resolute about who you are *not* targeting. A business with a clear brand strategy will find it easier to maintain this resolve: as Southwest Airline's CEO Herb

---

[1] This example is given by C.C. Markides in his book *All The Right Moves*. Harvard Business School Press, 1999.

Kelleher puts it: 'The customer is frequently wrong. We don't carry those sorts of customers. We write to them and say: "Fly somebody else".'[2]

- *Tough decisions: what do we sell?*
  Intel is no stranger to taking tough decisions. In the early 1980s the company abandoned manufacturing computer memory, choosing instead to focus on microprocessors. However, within two years the company faced another difficult choice: whether to continue with its existing CISC technology, or back the new RISC approach. The internal debates were ferocious, and divided the company. Unable to resolve the dispute, the company hedged its bets – it backed both technologies. However, the results were nearly disastrous: time and resources within Intel were split, and the company's energies were focused on an internal struggle between two visions of the future. It soon became clear to Intel's CEO, Andrew Grove, that the company had lost its answer to the question *'What do we sell?'*[3] A decision was needed: Groves withdrew from the RISC technology, and refocused the company behind CISC – a decision that paved the way for Intel's subsequent well-known success.

FINDING A NEW DEFINITION OF THE MARKET

We've already introduced the Market Definition Cycle (above), which illustrates how the questions *'Who is our customer?'* and *'What do we sell?'* cannot be answered in isolation from each other. A brand can find answers to these questions by using a straightforward 'generate and test' methodology – or, as Intel's Andrew Grove puts it, 'Let chaos reign, then reign in chaos'.[4]

---

[2] See footnote 1.

[3] Andrew Grove discusses this in his book *Only the Paranoid Survive*. Harper Collins, 1997.

[4] Andrew S. Grove, 'A high-tech CEO updates his views on managing and careers', *Fortune* (18 September 1995).

1. Generate: let chaos reign

Chaos is defined as 'a condition of great disorder or confusion'.[5] While many businesses devote much of their energy to avoiding this state, it's a necessary part of finding creative answers: the most powerful market definitions are those that are not obvious and that no one else has thought of.

The first step is to think creatively, to identify all the possible answers – no matter how absurd they may seem at first. Imagine the people who might possibly buy your product, and all the possible products you might sell to your customers. Discover all of the different ways that your product might be used, and imagine the many different needs your customers might have. The framework in Figure 15.2 can act as a guide to generating answers, bringing together the *'who?'* and the *'what?'* questions.

As this framework shows, there are four possible approaches a brand can take to find a new definition of the market:

- Existing products can be exploited in existing, known markets – such as new demographic groups, or new country markets.
- New (or latent) customer needs may be uncovered, by finding new uses for existing products. This often happens in the pharmaceuticals business – for example, aspirin was found to have strong de-clotting properties, and thus accessed a new market.

WHO ?

WHAT ?	**Existing needs**	**New needs**
Existing products	Find new possible markets for existing products (e.g. launch of product in new country market, such as Axe in the US)	Find possible new uses of existing products (e.g. Lucozade (a glucose convalescent drink) becoming an 'energy' youth drink)
New products	Find new possible products for existing markets (e.g. launch of Gillette Mach 3 to the men's shaving market)	Find possible new products that meet latent customer needs (e.g. 3M Post-It notes uncovered a latent need to stick small notes everywhere)

Figure 15.2 *Framework for generating new market definitions*

[5] *The American Heritage® Dictionary of the English Language*, Fourth Edition. Copyright © 2000 by Houghton Mifflin Company. Published by Houghton Mifflin Company. All rights reserved.

- New (or latent) customer needs may be uncovered, and new products developed to meet them. For example, Sony Walkman uncovered a latent market for listening to music while moving around.
- New products may be developed for existing markets – for example, innovative new products in established markets (such as Gillette's Mach 3) or new products in markets with high wear-out potential (such as films or books).

2. Test: reign in chaos

Having generated lots of possible market definitions for the brand – and lots of answers to the questions 'who?' and 'what?' – we need to decide which to pursue, and which to reject. In other words, we need a clear set of criteria that can be applied. The following questions may act as a useful guide – if the answer to any one of these questions is 'no', the business should probably reject the proposed market definition:

- Does this market definition build on our overall brand position?
- Is this a potentially profitable market definition?
- Will this market definition contribute to employee motivation and satisfaction?
- Is this market definition aligned with our core competencies?

These questions may not provide a final answer about how to define the market – but they are certainly useful in dismissing inappropriate definitions. For example, the management of a leading UK newspaper company had been asking themselves the 'what?' question. They defined a new potential market: providing one- or two-day courses on 'hot' managerial issues to senior executives. A partnership proposal was written, and taken to the London Business School: the newspaper would market the course, and the LBS would design and deliver it.

The newspaper's management had undoubtedly defined a real, lucrative market – but the LBS declined to take part. We can assess their reasoning using the criteria above. While the opportunity may have been potentially profitable, and while employees may well have enjoyed running the courses, not all of the criteria were met. Offering short 'hot topic' courses did not build on the LBS's brand position as a serious academic institution, and was not aligned with the LBS's core competency of providing intensive and rigorous education and research.

The LBS was able to reject this proposal at an early stage, because it was clearly incompatible with the criteria laid down. However, sometimes this assessment is difficult to make, and can only be properly answered with the help of research, or even a trial launch. For really innovative products that deliver to latent consumer needs, even research and trial may not provide a conclusive answer. For example, when Sony first put its Walkman into trial, the results were very negative: many people couldn't see why they would want to listen to music unless they were comfortably sitting at home. In cases like these, the business needs to have the courage of its convictions.

16

Strategic Challenges

Different brands face different challenges at different times – this much is evident. A new brand launching into an emerging market will need a very different approach from an established brand operating in a mature market. How are we to make sense of these different challenges?

Long-standing brands such as IBM, Ford and Kodak all seem to have gone through distinct periods of growth, maturity, decline and transformation. We can see similar patterns in long-standing industries such as radio and rail travel. These observations have led many people to think of the strategic challenges facing brands in terms of *life cycles*. The predominant model is the *product life cycle*, which was popularized in the 1960s by Theodore Levitt.[1]

THE PRODUCT LIFE CYCLE

The concept of a product life cycle has become an established model in marketing. Most accounts of the theory divide the development of a product into four distinct phases, as outlined in Figure 16.1, The strategic challenge facing the business – and hence the objectives facing the brand – are taken to depend upon which phase of the product life cycle. In the *Introductory* phase the product struggles to gain acceptance with

---

[1] T. Levitt, 'Exploit the product life cycle', *Harvard Business Review*, Vol. 43, 81–94, 1965.

Introduction
Aggressive entry into market
Focus on performance and awareness

Growth
Maximize shares
Establish brand image / differentiation

Maturity
Defend share / maintain margins
Explore growth options, e.g. line extensions

Decline
Milk remaining segments
Rationalize product range / cut costs

Figure 16.1   *Product life cycle*

consumers, and the role of marketing is to build awareness and establish the performance of the product.

In the *Growth* phase the brand takes on a central role. As competitors enter the market, the strategic challenge is to maximize market share – and establishing a strong brand position becomes a focus for the business. During this phase the market begins to segment, and different groups of consumers emerge with different requirements.

As the market moves towards *Maturity*, sales reach their peak and competition intensifies: competitors pursue growth by targeting each other's customers. During this phase, a strong brand can help to consolidate market share. Price wars are a common feature of mature markets, and strong brands may help to support a price premium. The business may also seek to exploit the brand's strength by moving into new business areas.

The product life cycle enters its *Decline* phase as a new generation of products begin to enter the market. Sales decline, and competitors start to exit the market. A small core of brands may remain to supply the remaining customers. This phase may persist for some time, as the remaining customer base slowly dwindles.

This theory of how markets develop has had a major impact on marketing. Numerous variations on these four stages have been incorporated into business theory – such as Boston Consulting Group's Matrix, which describes the growth of a product using the following four labels:

Problem Child	low share of a high growth market
Star	high share of a high growth market
Cash Cow	high share of a low growth market
Dog	low share of a low growth market

This kind of approach proved useful for managing brand portfolios. Thus Boston Consulting Group boasts not unfairly: 'So great was the initial success of BCG's matrix that for the greater part of two decades it became the standard approach to capital allocation in multisector, multisegment companies'.[2]

The product life cycle approach was not without its detractors – not least because it seemed to focus on the product, and pay insufficient attention to customers. If products have life cycles, it must be because customers change their behaviours. How can we account for this? At roughly the same time as the product life cycle theory was taking shape, an account of customer behaviour was emerging.

DIFFUSION OF INNOVATION

Whether it's farmers trying a new variety of seed, consumers buying a new type of washing powder, kids playing a new console game, or management trying a new best practice, there's a common pattern to the way new products, ideas or practices are adopted. This was first recognized in a landmark book by Everett Rogers, published in 1962, called *Diffusion of Innovation*.

In his book, Rogers looked at an astonishing breadth of research, including anthropology, agriculture, public health, marketing, management and economics. His case studies covered such exotic topics as techniques for controlling scurvy in the British navy, to water boiling in Peruvian villages. By drawing together such a wide range of sources, Rogers was able to establish a robust pattern for the take-up of innovations.

Roger's theory is in parallel to the product life cycle. He divides the stages in the spread of innovation into four key phases: innovators, early

---

[2] www.bcg.com.

adopters, majority and laggards. Although these were defined separately from the product life cycle, these phases can be thought of as mapping onto the phases of introduction, growth, maturity and decline, respectively. Table 16.1 describes each of Roger's phases (he later divided Majority into 'early' and 'late'):

Table 16.1   Diffusion of innovation

Phase	% of Market	Description
Innovators	2.5%	Highly curious, driven by discovery Creative, experimental May have higher disposable incomes
Early Adopters	13.5%	Information-seekers, will read reviews and reports Opinion leaders, 'in the know' Interested in performance, return on investment
Early Majority	34%	Pragmatic, wants to see a track record Will often wait until there are competitive products Risk-averse, interested in value and convenience
Late Majority	34%	Conservative, prefer familiarity, seek trust Word of mouth/personal recommendation is key Don't want to get left behind
Laggards	16%	Attracted by falling prices Under-confident, need support and reassurance Fringe of the market, e.g. don't really need a PC

PRACTICAL IMPLICATIONS

These theories of how a market develops provide a very useful perspective on the many different challenges that may face a brand. However, we should be aware of their limitations.

- There's no definite way of pin-pointing which phase we are in. Of course, everyone has hunches and intuitions about this, but there are considerable grey areas between the phases – between innovator and early adopter, for example, or between introduction and growth.
- Different industries have very different characteristics. Products that are the result of intensive investment in R&D – such as pharmaceuticals – may remain unprofitable until the market matures. Other products may be profitable very quickly.
- Consumer behaviour often defies prediction. Countless fads and fashions illustrate that people often adopt and reject products in highly unexpected ways. For example, a product may be adopted by an unintended consumer group – such as the widespread adoption of GPS satellite positioning by Muslims looking to find the direction of Mecca. Also, consumer interest in a product may suddenly pick up during a period of managed decline.

These factors make it difficult to use the product life cycle theory as a strategic planning tool – although it may provide a general background perspective. Given this limitation, we find it more useful to think in terms of the types of strategic challenge that a brand may face (see p. 93). We shall now examine each of these challenges in more detail.

17

Launch

All new brand launches share one crucial fact: they are all highly likely to fail. Of course, businesses don't usually undertake new ventures in the belief that they will fail – but most studies agree that failure rates for new products are very high: around 80% for consumer goods, and around 30% for other types of brands. The period of time surrounding a brand launch is perhaps the most critical time in the life of any brand. Launching a new brand is the toughest challenge for any marketer.

WHY LAUNCH A NEW BRAND?

New brands are launched either to capture an opportunity or to respond to a threat. Here are some common factors that may lead businesses to launch a new brand:

- A new brand may introduce a new market – e.g. Amazon were the first online book retailer, and the name remains synonymous with its market.
- A new brand may herald a dramatic improvement in a well-defined product market – e.g. Dyson's bag-free vacuum cleaners, named after their inventor James Dyson.
- A new brand may represent a completely new approach to a market – e.g. EasyJet, which pioneered the no-frills budget airline sector in the UK.

- A new brand may engage an untapped consumer segment – e.g. American Express launched the Blue card to bring in younger customers not attracted by the Green card.
- A new brand may be launched as part of a rationalization of an overall portfolio – e.g. Ford's launch of the *Focus* to replace the weary *Escort* brand.
- A new brand may block a threat from competitors – e.g. Anheuser-Busch launched a number of beers (such as ZiegenBock) to counter the growing number of 'craft beer' brands.

Of course, before any new brand is launched the market must be clearly and insightfully defined, as discussed in Chapter 15. As a quick recap, a list of questions is given below: no brand launch should proceed until these questions are comprehensively answered.

ESSENTIAL QUESTIONS

1. Why does the world need this brand?
2. Who are the competitors – near and far?
3. How does this brand differ from competitors?
4. Who are the customers for this brand?
5. Who are NOT the customers for this brand?
6. What exactly is the product/service this brand will offer?
7. What is the 'know-how' of this brand?
8. What is this brand *NOT*?
9. Are the company's processes aligned behind the brand?
10. Can employees articulate the answer to question 1?

SELECTING A NAME FOR THE BRAND

Obviously, every new brand needs a name – and before we look at standard approaches to selecting a name, it's worth bearing in mind a cautionary tale about the brand name *Yahoo!*. Consider the following remarks, made in 1999:

You might have a provocative, fun name, but do you have the basis for a lasting brand? We still don't know how compelling a brand *Yahoo!* will be 10 years from now. I sense a real missed opportunity.

These comments were made by a leading naming expert from one of the world's largest naming agencies – and they've been proved decisively wrong: the *Yahoo!* name has clearly set the brand apart from their clone-like competitors, all of whom had highly descriptive names such as Infoseek, LookSmart, FindWhat, GoTo, etc. Far from a 'missed opportunity', Yahoo! is now established as one of the most successful brands on the internet.

There are two lessons we might draw from this. Firstly, there are no hard-and-fast rules about naming (or indeed about branding) – even the most seasoned experts can get it glaringly wrong. Secondly, selecting a name is only a part of building a brand: the real success of Yahoo! lies in the energy and commitment of its founders David Filo and Jerry Yang, who started the directory as a student hobby and transformed it into a substantial business.

Filo and Yang had very clear ideas about the name of their brand – but things aren't always this clear. If you're charged with launching a new range of vitamin supplements, or a new model of car – or perhaps even a new naming agency – how do you go about selecting a name? Before the naming process begins, the company should be able to answer the following questions:

- *What is the product and/or service?* For example, is it an innovative new product, part of a range, etc.?
- *Who is the customer?* For example, what are their specific needs and interests which this brand will satisfy?
- *What is the brand's position?* For example, how will a customer think of this brand, in relation to competitors?
- *What is the long-term vision for the brand?* For example, does the brand hope to expand into other business areas?

The name-generation process may be done by a naming agency or internally – either way, the company should be able to answer these questions confidently before naming begins.

TYPES OF BRAND NAME

- *Descriptive names*

  These are the most straightforward type of brand name – it says what it does. Classic examples include *Rent-O-Kill*, *Post-It* and *Etch-A-Sketch*, *Pizza Express* and *Matchbox Cars*. Descriptive names are not ideal for brands that are intended to cross national borders: names like *Head and Shoulders* may resonate with English-speaking consumers as a name for an anti-dandruff shampoo, but this may be lost on non-English speakers.

- *Associative names*

  A brand name can be suggestive of the brand position. Sometimes this is done simply, though the use of an associated word: *Comfort* and *Snuggle* are both excellent names for fabric softeners. *Neutrogena* has semi-clinical overtones – it's derived from the words *neutral* and *hygiene*, and this lends further associations to the brand. The name *Slinky* seems to describe the smooth movement and sound of the toy. The name *Silkience* supports the shampoo's position as the essence of silkiness. However, like descriptive names, associative names also suffer from translation difficulties: *Silkience* is called *Soyance* in France, *Sientel* in Italy, and *Silience* in Germany.

- *Appropriated names*

  Brand names can be plundered from anywhere. Greek, for example: *Eidos* means 'form', *Xerox* is based on the word 'dry', *Omega* is of course the last letter of the Greek alphabet, and everyone knows that *Nike* was the Greek goddess of speed. However, none of this necessarily means much to consumers (few of whom are likely to know the Greek word for 'form'), and a brand launch must bring meaning to words such as this. Other appropriated names are more evocative: The mineral water *Vittel* takes its name from its town of origin in France, but the name suggests vitality. *Schweppes* is of course just a family name with no inherent meaning – but its name conveys the sound of effervescence. Indeed, Schweppes have made use of their name as an advertising concept, such as the famous 'Sch . . . you know who' campaign.

- *Invented names*

  Exxon, Lego, Kodak, Tampax, Zantac, Enron, Zeneca, Lucent, Kotex, Polaroid, Pepsi, Viagra, Cellophane and *Nylon* – the list of successful invented names is impressive, and notable for the high number of Z, X and hard K sounds (the five least common initial letters in English are X, Z, Y, Q and K – all of which are well represented in our random sample!) The challenge for lauching an invented brand name is far more than choosing the name: these are made-up words, empty of meaning, and the brand communications must work harder to give them meaning.

DON'T OVERLOOK THE ROLE OF PUBLICITY

For many businesses that are launching a new brand, the first impulse is *advertise*. Surely the first thing a new brand needs is awareness? Well, brand strategy is more than awareness, as we saw in Chapter 2. But what better way of creating associations for a new brand than through an anthemic TV campaign? Consumers generally have a habit of making their own minds up about new brands, rather than just accepting what they're told. Of course, advertising may play a vital role in a new brand launch, but it's often most effective when preceded by a publicity campaign.

Take, for example, the famous 'Think small' campaign for Volkswagen in the 1960s: legend has it that the advertising agency Doyle Dane Bernbach took a virtually unknown brand and made it into an overnight success. In fact, the VW had been selling healthy numbers in the US for more than a decade before this campaign ran – and by 1959 it was the biggest selling imported car, with almost 120 000 units sold. The press was full of favourable stories about the car – its styling and reliability. As powerful as the advertising was, it didn't *create* the brand: it took the emerging ideas created by publicity and gave them a strong identity and momentum. As Al Ries and Laura Ries succinctly put it: 'Publicity is the nail, advertising is the hammer.'[1]

---

[1] Al Ries and Laura Ries, 'First do some great publicity', *Advertising Age* – from where the details of this account are taken.

DON'T OVERLOOK THE ROLE OF WORD-OF-MOUTH

What consumers say to each other about a new brand will often make the difference between success and failure. Often, the key to generating positive word of mouth is to *pace the market*: to let consumers 'discover' the brand rather than ramming it down their throats with heavy advertising campaigns. Companies that can afford expensive launch campaigns often make the mistake of over-hyping a new brand: the surest way of generating *negative* word of mouth is to over-promise and under-deliver. The following three comparisons illustrate that generating a natural consumer 'buzz' can sometimes be more effective than big-budget 'hype'.

- *Buzz vs Hype #1: Big Brother vs Survivor*
  When the UK TV show *Big Brother* launched in 2000, its marketers based their launch strategy on the insight that people like to feel they've 'discovered' a TV show. They undertook a 'gently-gently' approach, building up press activity as interest grew. In contrast, the rival show *Survivor* undertook a massive pre-launch PR push: in the week before launch, *Survivor* achieved 131 press mentions, whereas *Big Brother* had only 79. After a slow start, *Big Brother* clearly emerged as the show everyone was talking about, and easily beat *Survivor*'s ratings. As one of the *Big Brother* marketing team put it, 'the massive hype [of *Survivor*] squashed the natural excitement for the show'.

- *Buzz vs Hype #2: Momenta vs Palm*
  'Our mantra was "Under-promise and over-deliver"' says Ed Colligan, former VP of marketing at Palm Computing, explaining the company's strategy for generating positive word of mouth. The success of Palm Pilot is well known, but it's worth remembering that it was in fact beaten to market by a sleek-looking hand-held computer called Momenta. Much excitement was generated by Momenta's massive advertising and PR push (it appeared on the cover of eight US magazines), but the product was slow and didn't meet the enormous expectation created by the advertising. By contrast, the Palm Pilot launched with little fuss and to low expectations – and because the product over-delivered, its best marketers were its own customers.

- *Buzz vs Hype #3: Blair Witch Project vs Godzilla*
  The success of the *Blair Witch Project* is a famous example of how positive word of mouth can outperform even the strongest of marketing muscles. The director of the film used the internet to create rumours about the content of the film. A year before the film's release there were 20 unofficial websites about the *Blair Witch Project*, and a considerable amount of speculation and buzz. On release, the film became a summer box office smash, eclipsing the much-hyped movie *Godzilla*, with its $200 million marketing spend.

IDENTIFY OPINION LEADERS

All opinions are not created equal. In almost every field of activity, individuals exist whose opinions carry more weight – usually because they've accumulated more knowledge on a subject, either through interest, experience, or sheer obsession. Everyone knows someone to ask if they need car advice, or a restaurant recommendation, or a point of view on the latest digital accessory. These individuals influence the behaviours and attitudes of others: for a new brand, their endorsement can be critical.

Pharmaceutical companies such as GSK were among the first to make use of opinion leaders. An early study into the subject asked physicians in the US Midwest to name colleagues whom they would ask for advice on treatments. The results showed that a small number of names came up repeatedly: clearly, these individuals were opinion formers.[2] GSK has incorporated these findings into its working practices. 'Key Opinion Leaders', as they are known to GSK, are formally identified and involved from an early stage in development of new drugs.

This kind of approach has been widely adopted in many sectors – from fashion, food and drink, to financial services. A whole industry of trend-spotters and 'cool-hunters' has evolved to glean insights from these opinion leaders, and to stimulate the 'networks of buzz' when the time comes to launch the new brand. 'Cool-hunting', as it sounds, is hardly a

---

[2] H. Menzel and J.S. Coleman in *Reports and Monographs of the Bureau of Applied Social Research*, New York: Clearwater Pub. Co. c1981. 807 fiches.

precise art. As Malcolm Gladwell puts it, 'the trick is not just to be able to tell who is different but to be able to tell when that difference represents something truly cool. It's a gut thing. You have to somehow know.'[3]

'It's a gut thing' doesn't exactly sound like a watertight formula for success. How exactly do we identify these opinion leaders? Well, as Gladwell suggests, there's no proper procedure for spotting them. However, a few common-sense guidelines apply:

- *Talk to professional experts.* Many people have jobs that provide them with well-informed opinions – and a position of influence. Examples include journalists, editors, shop assistants, hairdressers and dentists, When launching a new brand, these people may provide useful insights for brand planning, as well as stimulating word-of-mouth.

- *Find fanatics and obsessives.* Some products and brands inspire legions of devotees – for example, Apple Computers has a well-developed community of fans, and the company makes good use of these to spread the word about new products. Many categories – particularly entertainment, fashion and technology – have enthusiasts who can be used to stimulate word-of-mouth for a new brand launch.

- *Identify high-value customers.* Sometimes those who spend the most on a brand will be opinion formers, because of their greater experience of the category. For example, frequent fliers will have well-informed opinions about travel, and their endorsement can be helpful when launching a new brand.

DEVELOP A 'SEEDING' CAMPAIGN

Having identified our opinion leaders, what do we do with them? For anyone to form an opinion on a new product or service it usually helps if they've tried it. This is an essential step in building a new brand: putting the product in the hands of opinion leaders – often referred to as a 'seeding' campaign. Here are some examples:

---

[3] Malcolm Gladwell, 'The coolhunt', quoted in D. Lewis and D. Bridger, *The Soul of the New Consumer*, Nicholas Brieley, 2000.

- When launching a new model, car companies such as Ford may identify thousands of opinion leaders and offer to lend them a car for the weekend – a combination of sampling and flattery that's bound to generate word-of-mouth.
- When Trivial Pursuit launched in 1984 it sent samples to celebrities who were mentioned in the game – spawning 'trivia parties' in Hollywood, which themselves were sampling opportunities: the game's popularity became contagious.
- Publishers will regularly launch a new book with a seeding campaign. For a big launch, thousands of copies may be sent to opinion leaders – not just reviewers, but key people within the subject area who may make personal recommendations.
- In the early days of Apple, the company donated a computer to every school in California – generating much interest among students, teachers and parents alike – as well as giving the company a positive image for involvement in the community.

> To establish ourselves in the world, we have to do all we can to appear established. To succeed in the world, we do everything we can to appear successful.[4]
>
> The primary role of advertising is to say who you are.[5]
>
> If you can, be first. If you can't be first, create a new category in which you can be first.[6]
>
> The best way for a new brand to succeed is to act like an old brand.[7]
>
> You can't build a reputation on what you are going to do.[8]

[4] Francois la Rochefoucauld.

[5] Don Hudler, 'VP Marketing, Saturn', in Adam Morgan, *Eating the Big Fish*. John Wiley & Sons, 1999.

[6] Al Ries and Jack Trout, *The 22 Immutable Laws of Marketing*. Harper Collins, p. 33, 2002.

[7] Stephen King, *Developing New Brands*, John Wiley & Sons, 1973.

[8] Henry Ford.

18

Challenge

BIG BRANDS ARE GETTING BIGGER

Modern markets are dominated by a small number of big businesses. Two companies (Coke and Pepsi) prevail over the world's soft drinks market; one corporation (Microsoft) has a near monopoly on the world's operating systems; five companies (Exxon, Chevron, Texaco, BP and Shell) control the bulk of global oil supplies. Two retailers (Wal-Mart and Kmart) dominate the US retail market. Four banks (NatWest, LloydsTSB, HSBC and Barclays) hold 75% of all UK current accounts.

Increasingly, market share has become concentrated into an ever smaller number of companies, and this has been partly brought about by an extended period of mergers and acquisitions.

- In media, TimeWarner bought CNN, and then AOL bought Time-Warner.
- In automotive, Ford bought Jaguar, Volvo and Land Rover; Daimler took over Chrysler; GM bought Saab, and parts of Subaru, Fiat and Daewoo.
- In pharmaceuticals, Smithkline Beecham and Glaxo Welcome merged to become GlaxoSmithKline, and Pfizer swallowed up Warner-Lambert and Pharmacia.

Across many industries, consolidation has placed more market power in the hands of fewer players. These prodigious companies enjoy significant advantages: they have formidable marketing and advertising budgets, and can usually win any price war (and if this fails, they can often eliminate rivals by acquiring them); they can call the shots with suppliers, who may depend upon their large orders (and if this fails, there's always backwards integration: buy the supplier); they enjoy influence over government policy, access to distribution, and can fund substantial R&D programmes.

SMALLER BRANDS SUFFER 'DOUBLE JEOPARDY'

As if this didn't place smaller brands at a sufficient disadvantage, there is also the 'double jeopardy' effect, first observed by Andrew Ehrenberg (for a further discussion see p. 74): A small brand, according to Ehrenberg, is punished twice for being small: 'It has fewer buyers, and these few buyers are somewhat less loyal.'[1] The example given in Table 18.1[2] is typical of this pattern.

The pattern is clear: the smaller a brand gets, the greater the rate of defection. There are, however, some notable exceptions: Mercedes has a small market share, yet the rate of defection is lower than might be expected, indicating that some other factors are at work. Seat loses slightly more customers than might be expected, indicating perhaps that market share is sliding. Overall, however, the pattern holds, and Ehrenberg and his colleagues have repeatedly demonstrated the same theme: smaller brands need to work harder just to stay in the same place.

A TOUCH OF MADNESS

Given the disadvantages facing smaller brands, it's hard enough just to remain viable, let alone overtake the mammoth market leaders. Yet that

---

[1] A. Ehrenberg and G. Goodhardt, 'Double jeopardy revisited, again', *Marketing Research*, Spring 2001.

[2] R. Colombo, A. Ehrenberg and D. Sabalava, 'Diversity in analyzing brand switching tables: The Car Challenge', *Canadian Journal of Marketing Research*.

Table 18.1 Brand switching for cars (France 1998)

Brand	Market share	% of customers switching to another brand
Renault	31	36
Peugeot	23	40
Citroen	12	45
VW	8	44
Ford	7	45
Fiat	6	54
GM	5	47
Rover	2	65
Seat	2	74
Mercedes	1	30
Volvo	1	52
BMW	1	54
Lada	1	60
Alfa	1	62

is the task that many brands have set for themselves – and remarkably many succeed. These so-called *challenger brands* use all manner of inventive tactics to dislodge the dominant brands, and we examine some of these in this section. But challengers don't have an easy task. As one commentator put it: 'Without courage and even a touch of madness, challenger brands simply wouldn't exist.'[3] So, why does anyone bother?

CHALLENGER BRANDS MAKE MORE MONEY

It's clear that successful challenger brands may reap substantial financial rewards: Orange, Ben & Jerry's, PlayStation and Virgin were all once chal-

---

[3] J. Kapfer *[Re]inventing the Brand*, Kogan Page, London, 2001.

lengers, and continue to have challenger-like attitudes. Further evidence comes from looking at new business launches. Of course, most launches are not challengers: the *Financial Times* undertook a study into 100 new launches and found that 86% of these were incremental improvements on existing products. The same study showed that those brands which ignored the prevailing assumptions about the market were far more successful: of all brands covered in the study, these challengers generated 38% of revenues and 61% of profits. Apparently, it pays to challenge. But, challenge *what* exactly?

CHALLENGE THE MARKET DEFINITION

In Chapter 15 we saw that defining the market is a key strategic task. Answering the questions '*Who are our customers?*' and '*What are we selling?*' can unlock powerful competitive advantages. This is particularly true for smaller brands seeking to win a better market position. The following examples show that it's possible to disrupt markets, without expensive advertising campaigns.

- When Interbrew launched the beer Hoegaarden in the UK, it had a fresh answer to the question, *Who are our customers?* Most beer brands cast their nets wide, targeting a broad range of consumers. Hoegaarden wanted to become a firm favourite among young, affluent 'opinion-forming' drinkers. To achieve this, the beer was only supplied to a small number of London's cooler bars. This was a powerful way of stimulating demand: around London, aspirational drinkers started asking for this trendy new brew – and within a year many of Interbrew's trade customers were insisting on stocking it.

Interbrew also asked themselves the question, *What are we selling?* At the time of launch, all beers in the UK were served in standard, unbranded pint glasses. Realizing the important role of appearance among these trend-conscious consumers, Interbrew introduced a new, branded glass for Hoegaarden (see Figure 18.1). This format was rigorously applied: teams of covert Hoegaarden drinkers were dispatched,

Figure 18.1   *Hoegaarden's branded glass (© Interbrew)*

and any bars found serving the beer in plain glasses would have their supply withdrawn.

• When the search engine Google was launched in 1998, the market for seeking information on the internet was dominated by Yahoo! – which was by this time a successful publicly-quoted company with a strong management line-up and dozens of web properties across the globe. Yahoo!'s market definition went something like this: provide internet users with a comprehensive guide to websites, selected by Yahoo! staff. Yahoo!'s dominance of the market seemed unassailable. Indeed, such was Yahoo!'s influence over people's activities on the internet that a 'Yahoo! Sucks' campaign sprang up, calling on people to boycott the company because it had become too powerful.

Against this background, Google offered a fresh approach. Instead of using editors or employees to judge a website's importance, Google searches the web and ranks the results in order of how popular they are. This new approach enabled Google to claim a superior morality: democracy. The brand's language is full of phrases like 'easy, honest and objective', 'uniquely democratic nature' and 'integrity'. This proved compelling for web users. By 2003 the company was processing 250 million searches a day, or 2900 searches a second, in 88 languages in

32 countries. Analysts estimate its revenues were about $300 million in 2002, when it delivered operating margins of 20% to 30%.

CHALLENGE THE MAINSTREAM

In established categories, consumers usually have fairly fixed preferences. They know what they like, they know what they don't like, and they don't question things too much. This is the mainstream: millions of consumers acting largely out of habit, and not giving their decisions too much thought. We all do it – and often with good reason: if we had to weigh up the emotional and rational benefits each time we wanted to buy a packet of crisps, life would become even more complicated. Habits have their place; the mainstream holds sway.

Challenging the mainstream is sometimes the only option for smaller brands. Consumers' habits must be unsettled if a hungry brand is to make headway. How can we force consumers to put off established preferences? A number of methods have been articulated in recent years, and two examples are given here.

- *Breakthrough ideas*
  Mark Blair and his colleagues at Ogilvy in Asia describe *breakthough ideas* as 'making the familiar strange, and the strange familiar'[4]. This, they argue, is how to get people to think differently about familiar, mainstream products. They give as an example the standard safety announcement given onboard an aircraft shortly before take-off. Having heard this many times before, most passengers take little notice. One airline, recognizing the need to get people's attention, set about 'making the familiar strange'. One of their official safety announcements runs like this: 'There may be 50 ways to leave your lover, but there are only six exits from this aircraft. We suggest you note their positions now.' (The airline, of course, is Southwest.)

---

[4] Mark Blair, Richard Armstrong and Mike Murphy, *The 360 Brand in Asia*, John Wiley & Sons, 2003.

- *Disruption*

  Jean Marie-Dru, president and CEO of TBWA, describes challenging the mainstream in terms of *disruption*: overturning convention in some way – perhaps through product innovation, brand positioning or communications. TBWA has a number of example brands which have disrupted their categories, including Apple, Absolut and PlayStation. When Sony launched PlayStation in 1995 it was third to market after Sega and Nintendo, which together commanded 97% of the market. PlayStation used hard-hitting imagery to overturn the convention that gaming was for kids and geeks. PlayStation's advertising conveyed the intensity of the gaming experience, with no age-limits, using the line 'Do not underestimate the power of the PlayStation!'

BEHAVIOURS OF SUCCESSFUL CHALLENGERS

A number of common behaviours can be seen in many successful challenger brands. In an extensive study, Adam Morgan identified eight common characteristics. He describes these in detail in his book *Eating the Big Fish,* a comprehensive account of challengers.

- In preparing for launch, successful challengers make a distinct break from their immediate past, establishing afresh the core issues facing the brand. Morgan notes that it is often newcomers to an industry that make the biggest impact, such as Richard Branson at Virgin, Michael Dell at Dell, and Ian Schrager in the hotel business.
- Instead of building their brands by talking about consumers ('because we understand your needs', etc.) or in relation to competitors ('better, stronger, longer', etc.), successful challengers build an identity that doesn't depend upon the world around them. Morgan gives as examples Diesel, Swatch, and Body Shop – as well as Las Vegas, whose brand position is, simply, 'Las Vegas is Las Vegas'.
- Instead of aiming to become market leaders in a category, successful challenger brands often aim to become *thought leaders*. For example, the mobile operator Orange, a late entrant into the UK cellular market, didn't once show a handset in its advertising – preferring to

paint an inspiring picture of 'a wirefree future' – and thus assuming thought leadership.

- Creating a 'symbol of re-evaluation' is a method used by some challengers to force reappraisal of their brand within the category. Morgan gives the example of Dodge, which launched the Viper – a loud, bright sports model – in order to shake consumers out of their perceptions of Dodge as a quiet, sensible brand.

- Successful challengers aren't afraid to polarize consumers. Some of Fox's most successful programming – such as *The Simpsons* and *The X-Files* contained content which turned-off large numbers of older, more conservative viewers. Fox sacrificed volume for the greater loyalty of a well-defined audience.

- Challengers must be prepared to over-commit, if they are to be successful. For example, shortly after launch, Lexus was forced to recall 8000 cars – a potential disaster for a brand based upon luxury and performance. Lexus turned this into a positive by over-committing to exceptional service standards, ensuring that repairs were done swiftly and – where possible – at the customer's home.

- Communications and advertising are used to become part of popular culture. For example, Absolut uses its highly stylized advertising – often by well-known artists – to attract press coverage and widespread interest (Absolut's campaigns have even been exhibited in art galleries). Publicity is key, particularly when budgets may be thin.

- The final observation Morgan makes about successful challenger brands is that they 'fly unstable' – i.e. they operate in an environment which constantly re-evaluates the core business issues and encourages new perspectives. A sense of drama helps: such as Steve Job's call-to-arms when Apple launched the flagship Macintosh computer: make or break within 100 days.

Without courage and even a touch of madness, challenger brands simply wouldn't exist.[5]

It's impossible to be too strong at the decisive point.[6]

Lack of money is no obstacle. Lack of an idea is an obstacle.[7]

The big do not always eat the little. The fast always eat the slow.[8]

An essential aspect of creativity is not being afraid to fail.[9]

Challenger is not really a series of actions but an underlying way of thinking.[10]

---

[5] J. Kapfer, [Re]inventing the Brand, Kogan Page, London, 2001.

[6] Napoleon.

[7] Ken Hakuta.

[8] The chairman of BMW Europe, 1989, in Adam Morgan, Eating the Big Fish. John Wiley & Sons, 1999.

[9] Dr Edwin Land.

[10] Adam Morgan, Eating the Big Fish. John Wiley & Sons, 1999.

19

Maintain

Many modern brands have real longevity: they've been around for a long, long time – yet still manage to stay up-to-date and relevant. For example, the famous signature logos of Kellogg's and Ford both date from 1906, and the three-pointed star of Mercedes Benz first appeared in 1926. Evian water has been bottled since 1826, and Coca-Cola's curves have been around since 1887. The Kodak brand name was invented in 1888 by George Eastman, who had a predilection for the letter K ('. . . it seemed a strong, incisive sort of letter'). The oil company Shell first used a shell motif in 1900. In 1917 the antiquely named Computing Tabulating-Recording Company became known as International Business Machines Co. Limited – and IBM was born. Even some of the great advertising agencies have veteran brands: J Walter Thompson appeared in 1877; Young & Rubicam was formed in 1923, and Ogilvy & Mather in 1948.

These are, of course, all exceptionally long-standing brands, spanning several generations. Most categories, however, are littered with the burnt wrecks of brands that have shone brightly but too briefly. The airline industry, for example, can count Pan Am, Eastern Airlines, Skytrain, TWA and Trump Shuttle among its more glorious failures – and that's before the downturn that hit the industry following the terrorist attacks of 9/11. Other than world events and massive market disruptions, there is one major reason that a brand may fail: consumers. They're a fickle lot: they may become bored and restless, they're easily tempted by shiny new things, their tastes change, their needs change, and finally they grow old and die. Little wonder it's so difficult to sustain a brand in the long term.

Added to the whimsical nature of consumers, brands operating in mature markets often face intense competition. Opportunities for growth in established categories are usually limited to stealing customers from the competition – and as a result there may be heavy pressure on price. Given all of these factors, it can often require the full energy and attention of a brand team just to defend market share and support price. It's rather like the observation made to Alice by the Red Queen in Lewis Carroll's *Through the Looking Glass*: 'in this place it takes all the running you can do, to keep in the same place.'

QUESTION THE BRAND STRATEGY

Successful companies must be continually vigilant against complacency and inertia – this has become received business-wisdom. Management guru Charles Handy speaks of 'the paradox of success': when things are going well there seems to be no reason to change – although this may be when the need for change is greatest.[1] Similarly, ex-Intel boss Andrew Grove talks about 'the inertia of success', and describes how businesses become resistant to changing the strategies that bought them success. Groves' book on this subject is aptly titled, *Only the Paranoid Survive*.[2]

If Chairman Mao had been the CEO of a major company, this kind of paranoid vigilance may have been his style. Instead, as leader of China he presided over a regime of 'constant reinvention'. Leon Trotsky's insistence on 'permanent revolution' makes him sound like a modern management guru (which may have been safer than being the leading critic of Stalin). In this respect, business is rather like politics: at times of success, the need for change may be greatest. As British statesman Lord Beaverbrook wrote: 'In the moment of supreme triumph, decline begins

---

[1] Charles Handy, *The Elephant and the Flea*. Arrow, 2002.
[2] Andrew Grove, *Only the Paranoid Survive*, HarperCollins, 1997.

to do its work.'[3] This is echoed by Andrew Grove: 'Business success contains the seeds of its own destruction.'[4]

History has many examples of great leaders who become a too confident in their power, while the conspirators are sharpening their knives. So it is in business: the story of yesterday's superstar company found stagnating and frustrated is a familiar one. However, too much questioning can be very destabilizing; too much paranoia can erode a company's resolve. Organizations that frequently shift their strategy may never really find their stride. So, when is the right time for a company to question its brand strategy?

Well, there is never a *wrong* time – but some times are more useful than others. There are broadly three phases during which a company might review its brand strategy, and these are described in Figure 19.1.

- *Crisis.* Cash-strapped and loss-making brands that are experiencing major problems may need to change direction in order to survive, but by this time it's probably too late. An ailing company finds it difficult to muster the resources and the confidence needed to implement an effective review of the brand strategy.

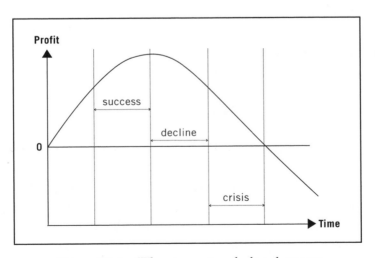

Figure 19.1 *When to question the brand strategy*

---

[3] Quoted in Jeremy Paxman, *The Political Animal*, Penguin Politics, 2002.
[4] See footnote 2.

- *Decline*. When sales and profits are falling – consistent with the symptoms of an outdated brand strategy – most businesses will start asking questions. However, the real competitive advantage will go to the company that spots the early warning signs of decline; ideally, this should be given some thought while the business is still profitable and sales are healthy.
- *Success*. Sustained growth and consistent profits are a sure signs that a business should start questioning its brand strategy. A successful company has the resources – though not always the inclination – to effectively review strategy and, if appropriate, implement change.

THE ROLE OF LEADERSHIP

When times are good, the average CEO's diary is packed with a disproportionate number of speeches to industry associations, meetings with executive staff, breakfasts with journalists, charity dinners, and travel. He or she may become preoccupied with pet projects, investments, acquisitions and talk of mergers. These matters can create a gravity of their own, leaving little time to worry about such mundane issues as the slipping sales in some minor distribution channel. Not so for Bill Gates, who can hardly be described as an 'average CEO', and who is said to have a pathological appetite for bad news. The role of leadership when times are good is to remain alert to signs that the brand strategy may need updating: few people in the company will have the perspective or the power to do anything about these signals.

When decline sets in, the average CEO may launch an aggressive hunt for operational efficiencies – maintaining margins by controlling costs. He or she may draft in the management consultants, who will install a regime of targets, benchmarking and best practice. However, often the problem is not how well the company is performing, but what the company is *doing*. This is the time to urgently ask the key questions of brand strategy, such as what products and services should we be offering, and to whom? For a company in decline, answering these questions may require some tough decisions. The role of leadership is to make these decisions, providing a clear strategy for the brand.

REVIEWING BRAND STRATEGY: TWO INTERVENTIONS

As we saw in chapter 2, there are four key questions that must be asked in order to define a brand strategy. These are as follows:

1. Who are our customers?
2. What products or services will we offer?
3. How will we compete with products or services from competitors?
4. What resources and capabilities do we need to deliver these products or services?

These are the questions to ask – but sometimes it takes more than a few questions to penetrate the organizational fug that can befall a substantial business. Sometimes, a disruption or intervention is needed. Two examples of such interventions follow.

Intervention #1: Positive crisis

Creating a crisis doesn't automatically sound like a sensible approach to maintaining a brand – but this is the approach described by the London Business School's Constantinos Markides. Markides gives a persuasive case for the need for disruption (he conceives of a company's organization as a *system*):

> Eventually, the system will reach a stage of 'blissful' stability, characterized by self-satisfaction, overconfidence or even arrogance, a strong but monolithic culture, a strong memory that allows the company to operate on auto-pilot, and strong internal political coalitions. Inevitably, success will breed unyielding mental models that in turn produce passive thinking . . . Every few years, then, something must happen to shock and destabilize the system all over again.[5]

This is Markides' argument for deliberately giving periodic, sudden shocks to a business. He gives examples of such shocks – which he calls *positive*

---

[5] Constantinos Markides, *All the Right Moves*, Harvard Business School Press, 2000.

crisis – citing General Electric's Jack Welch, who was not afraid to disrupt a smoothly running, successful business. In 1997, GE was posting record profits and the business looked in excellent shape. Welch's instinct was to destabilize the company before the fug descended, and he stunned observers by announcing a massive restructuring programme.

Intervention #2: Abandonment

Maintaining a brand in the long term sometimes requires the decision to *stop* certain activities – rather than make them more efficient. This includes everything from media and distribution deals, to product portfolios. As long-time management commentator Peter Drucker puts it: 'Nothing is less productive than to make more efficient what should not be done at all.'[6]

To address this, Drucker proposes a systematic and purposeful programme of *abandonment*: on a regular schedule, every product, every policy, every customer and partner must be put 'on trial for its life'. The organization must ask itself, 'If we did not do this already, would we be going into it now?' If the answer is '*no*' then the company's reaction should not be simply to commission another study – the organization must be committed to action. This approach, Drucker suggests, should be undertaken at least every three years. A number of companies now hold regular sessions to ask these questions – intriguingly called 'abandonment retreats'.

Drucker began thinking about abandonment while working with General Electric. When Jack Welch took over as CEO of GE in 1981, he invited Drucker to advise him on the single most important thing he could do to improve the company. As we have seen, Welch himself had an appetite for disruption – and Drucker's advice didn't disappoint him: if your products or services aren't number one or number two in the market, he told Welsh – kill them. This enabled Welch to focus the efforts of the GE into the real opportunities.

---

[6] Quoted in an interview with The Leadership Network, http://www.leadnet.org

ADAPT TO CHANGING TASTES AND NEEDS

Coca-Cola is often held up as the ultimate example of a steadfast, consistent brand with an unchanging product. For consumers, the New Coke fiasco in the 1980s only served to reinforce the perception that Coca-Cola has remained essentially unchanged for more than a century. Of course, there are many elements of the product and the brand that remain constant – but Coca-Cola has hardly remained unchanged. The company has continually responded to the changing preferences of its consumers, launching Diet Coke, caffeine-free coke, Lemon-flavoured coke, as well as numerous new formats – including PVC bottles, cans, on-tap mixes – and new points of consumption, most notably vending machines.

ALIGN THE BRAND'S LONG-TERM INTERESTS WITH THOSE OF SHAREHOLDERS

Brands need to develop competitive positions that are sustainable over the long term – yet this is bedevilled by the increasing focus on quarterly earnings. Coca-Cola is one of a number of companies that has stopped issuing quarterly earnings guidance to investors, in an attempt to foster a more long-term perspective of the company's performance. The interests of investors are often different from those of the brand: investors are quick to take profits, and increasingly likely to sell at the first whiff of bad news. Intel and Gillette are among other companies who have decided to withhold quarterly earnings guidance. As Coca-Cola CEO, Douglas Daft, explained: 'Establishing short-term guidance prevents a more meaningful focus on the strategic initiatives that a company is taking to build its business and succeed over the long run.'[7]

---

[7] Douglas Daft press release, 13 December 2003.

ALIGN THE BRAND'S LONG-TERM INTERESTS WITH THOSE OF CONSUMERS

There's an essential element of a brand's long-term success that is often taken for granted: the long-term well-being of its customers. Occasionally, the consequences of overlooking this seemingly obvious fact can be damaging. McDonald's, for example, encountered its first ever loss in the last quarter of 2002, as consumers became increasingly aware of the health problems associated with their particular variety of fast food. As the US burger market reached saturation in the late 1970s, so levels of obesity reached epidemic proportions. In the UK, the number of fast food outlets doubled between 1984 and 1993 – as did the prevalence of adult obesity.

The backlash has begun. Sales are down, as McDonald's and Burger King find themselves increasingly drawn into competing on price – a sure sign that the brands are losing their relevance. McDonald's has tried to respond by introducing new, healthier product lines – such as the McSalad Shaker and the McLean Deluxe. However, McDonald's and Burger King have built vast empires by anchoring their brands into the quick-fix sizzle of high-fat fast food. For too long these companies have neglected the real, long-term interests of their consumers. As a result, people may be slow to believe that McDonald's or Burger King really have their health at heart.

QUOTABLE QUOTES

Business success contains the seeds of its own destruction.[8]

In the moment of supreme triumph, decline begins to do its work.[9]

Every few years, something must happen to shock and destabilize the system all over again.[10]

Nothing is less productive than to make more efficient what should not be done at all.[11]

The day we think we've got it made, that's the day we'd better start worrying about going out of business.[12]

True loyalty cannot be bought; it needs to be inspired.[13]

We are so busy measuring public opinion that we forget we can mould it.[14]

Our biggest competitor is ourselves.[15]

---

[8] Andrew Grove, *Only the Paranoid Survive*, HarperCollins, 1997.

[9] Quoted in Jeremy Paxman, *The Political Animal*, Penguin Politics, 2002.

[10] Constantinos Markides, *All the Right Moves*, Harvard Business School Press, 2000.

[11] Quoted in an interview with The Leadership Network, http://www.leadnet.org

[12] Rick Teerlink, President, CEO, Harley-Davidson, quoted in Adam Morgan, *Eating the Big Fish*.

[13] *British Army Officer Training Manual* (in 360 Brand in Asia).

[14] Bill Bernbach.

[15] Manuel J. Cortez, CEO Las Vegas Visitors Authority, in Adam Morgan, *Eating the Big Fish*.

20

Revitalize

To *revitalize* means to 'impart new life, to bring vigor.'[1] Inner city slums are revitalized, as are ailing patients and flagging economies. Brands are revitalized when they lose their shine and the business starts to decline. Many brands experience this, although the decline of a brand is not inevitable. Despite frequent use of words like 'life cycle' and 'ageing', it's important to remember that brands are not biological entities: in principle, there's no reason why a brand should not continue indefinitely. However, for any long-running brand, there may be periods when fortunes turn sour and a period of crisis begins (see Figure 19.1).

There are many reasons a brand may fall into decline. Many of these are outlined in Chapter 19, which described how to maintain a brand over the long term. Some examples are given below.

- Fads may lead consumers away from a brand – for example, in 2003 the Atkin's low-carbohydrate diet craze dented Slim-Fast sales by an estimated 30%.
- Consumer tastes may change – for example, in the 1990s, a growing preference for new world Chardonnay was bad news for the German Riesling Blue Nun; similarly, a growing dislike of dark chocolate has been disastrous for UK brand Black Magic.
- Sometimes, changing tastes can be so extreme that even the brand's name sounds repulsive – for example, US brands Guycan Corned

---

[1] *The American Heritage® Dictionary of the English Language*, Fourth Edition.

Mutton or Hormel Potted Meat Product have an increasingly niche consumer base.

- Behaviours may change – for example, the increase of showering and a preference for shower gel dented sales of soap bar brands such as Imperial Leather, who were forced to launch shower gel variants.
- Changes in the market structure may spell doom for a brand – for example, the UK magazine *TV Times* entered a severe decline after government deregulation made TV listings available to all magazines.

A brand facing this kind of crisis has the following choices: it may attempt to turn around its fortunes – through repositioning, innovation, communications or even renaming – or it may accept its trajectory into a small niche brand, facing possible extinction.

In some of these examples – for example, Imperial Leather – revitalization is possible through repositioning and new product launch. Some brands might require a renaming in order to shake off their associations with dated preferences. For others – for example, the delightfully named Bile Beans (Figure 20.1) – it's difficult to imagine how a real revitalization might ever take place.

KNOWING WHEN TO SAY GOODBYE

Despite the best efforts of brand planners, a brand may sometimes become an anachronism. Bob's Quality Kraut Juice, for example, has a small but loyal following among senior citizens in Mississippi, who use it as a laxative. Unfortunately, this brand's days may be numbered: kraut juice is less than popular among younger consumers. According to one account, 'it smells like a cross between a malfunctioning septic tank and a poorly ventilated poultry farm.'[2]

Brands such as this face a tough decision: try to reverse the decline – entailing further investment communications and product development – or abandon the brand altogether and concentrate resources elsewhere. Many brands have faced this decision: Moulinex, Hoffmeister, Crest,

---

[2] Paul Lukas, *Inconspicuous Consumption*, Random House.

Figure 20.1   *Bile Beans – revitalization might be a challenge*

Ovaltine, Oldsmobile, Brut, Old Spice, Firestone, Brylcreem, Burma Shave, Breck, SunSilk, Care Bears and Soda Stream, to name a few. How does a business decide whether to invest further resources in a declining brand? The first step is to identify the problem.

IDENTIFY THE PROBLEM

There are many factors that motivate and influence a consumer's decision to buy a brand, and these change over time. The decline of a brand is always due to a failure to keep up these changes. Several factors may be involved:

- *Taste factors*. As we've seen, tastes may change between generations. For example, when it was launched, Camay's pink and flower-scented soap bar was a luxurious contrast to the caustic soda soaps that preceded it – although subsequent generations found it sickly and artificial, and sales slumped. Product development revitalized the brand, which now describes its scent as 'sexy, exotic'.

- *Cultural factors.* A brand's decline may be the effect of changing cultural influences – from religion, nationality, or social class. For example, when sugar cubes were introduced they were embraced by the English upper classes as the height of refinement (silver tongs were produced for their elegant dispatch into cups of tea). However, as they became cheaper, sugar cubes could be found in roadside cafes and working-class kitchens – and thus were soon regarded as 'common' by the upper classes. Now, sugar cubes are a marginal product.

- *Social factors.* Brands are often used to signal an individual's membership of a social group, or the role or status in society. This can apply to many categories – including cars, clothes, running shoes and choice of beer. For example, in the 1990s, Porsche entered a period of decline when the brand came to symbolize the brash, greedy yuppies of the 1980s.

- *Relevance factors.* Changes in people's behaviours or in technologies may quickly render a brand irrelevant. For example, the growth of air travel in the US caused the inevitable decline of the once-mighty railroad industry. A brand's decline may be linked to other consumption habits: for example, the decline of stock cube sales in the UK was a result in falling meat consumption.

BE HONEST: ADDRESS THE PROBLEM HEAD ON

Declining brands are likely to suffer from a lack of credibility. They may find it difficult to arouse much interest in anything they say or do. Consumers are likely to respond with cynicism, or worse – indifference. In order to make any impact, declining brands must be bold – and one of the boldest things any brand can do is *be honest*. If a brand has a troubled history, acknowledging this is the first step to repairing its image.

This approach was behind one of the most remarkable turnarounds ever seen in the UK. The brand involved was Skoda – a much maligned car, known to British consumers as the laughably unreliable product of Soviet bloc engineering. So unfortunate was the brands reputation that it spawned a whole genre of laughably bad jokes (e.g. 'What do you call a Skoda with twin exhaust?', 'A wheelbarrow'). This was the situation facing Skoda in the early 1990s: a brand famous for its poor quality.

If ever there was a brand in need of revitalization, this was it. The turn-around began with the collapse of communism, which enabled a partnership between Skoda and Volkswagen. But having addressed the quality issues, the brand needed to address consumer opinion – which was still stacked heavily against it. Even industry awards for Skoda's new model – the Fabia – did not change consumers' minds. A review in *The Mirror*, a leading UK newspaper, summed it up:

> I see the Fabia has been named 'Car of the Year' but I don't think I'm ready to drive one yet. I still think it's less embarrassing to be seen getting out of the back of a sheep than getting out of the back of a Skoda.
>
> *The Mirror* (February 2000)

The task of turning around consumer opinion was taken on by the advertising agency Fallon, who were determined to tackle the problem head-on. They describe the task as follows: 'Our story is in some ways an old-fashioned case of "only advertising can do this", as this brand's very public problem demanded broadcast – as opposed to private – communication.'[3]

The campaign was bold indeed: 'It's a Skoda. Honest' (Figure 20.2) acknowledged directly the incredulity awaiting the launch of the new models: the car was so good-looking, so well-engineered, that people simply won't believe it's a Skoda. The idea was executed with gentle self-mocking humour. One TV ad featured a worried parking attendant: 'I'm very sorry sir, but some little vandal has stuck a Skoda badge on your car.' The campaign was very well received, and apart from numerous industry awards, achieved an astonishing turnaround for the brand. Skoda reached 61% of its year's target in three months, and the manufacturer suddenly found it had a 1500-strong waiting list for the first time in the company's

---

[3] L. Green and F. Morgan, 'It's a Skoda, Honest', IPA paper.

Figure 20.2   *A print ad from the 'It's a Skoda. Honest' campaign*

history. Between 1999 and 2001, UK Skoda sales increased by 64%. *The Mirror* newspaper described Skoda's change in fortunes as 'history's biggest comeback since Bobby Ewing stepped out of the shower; new Skoda is hip and sexy – yes, sexy' (*The Mirror*, March 2002).

FORCE RE-EVALUATION THROUGH PRODUCT DEVELOPMENT

In the late 1980s Chrysler was in the midst of an extensive period of stagnation: the brand had lost its shine with consumers, and the company had failed to produce any new break-through models. As a result, Chrysler's future was looking uncertain, and the management faced pressure to cut costs. What the company desperately needed, observers said, was a high-volume, mid-range model – a cash cow. However, the company's CEO, Bob Lutz, chose a very different direction. He backed the development of a high-performance, low-volume sports car – whose nearest neighbours were the Porsche 911, Mustang Cobra and Corvette Z06.

And so Chrysler opened a new chapter in its history when the Dodge Viper concept car was first shown in 1989. This would be Chrysler's 'halo car', forcing consumers to re-evaluate the brand. It would be a throwback to the head-turning sports cars of old: muscular, noisy, and very fast. Even if the Viper is a little over-boned for the average suburban Dad, other

Chrysler marques could bask in its reflected glory. It worked, and a turn-around began: within four years Chrysler was declaring record earnings. Lutz describes the role of the car:

> . . . the Viper gave us the forward momentum we desperately needed, both internally and externally with the financial community, the automobile magazines, and all of those constituencies that create the psychological climate in which your company either prospers or doesn't.[4]

---

[4] Bob Lutz, interviewed by Alden M. Hayashi, *Harvard Business Review*, 00178012, February 2001, Vol. 79, Issue 2.

21

Re-brand

Sometimes, a business may seek to change direction so fundamentally that the old brand is an irrelevance – or worse, a hindrance. Sometimes re-branding may follow a merger or de-merger, an acquisition or a spin-off. Sometimes, a company may seek to rationalize its portfolio of brands, or harmonize its brands in different country markets. Re-branding may be prompted by a crisis or scandal, or a brand may simply need a fresh start – sometimes, trying to revitalize an old brand that's lost its shine is like polishing the proverbial turd.

Re-branding may take several forms, ranging from changes of name and changes in imagery (visual symbols and colours, auditory mnemonics, etc.) to redefining the brand strategy and positioning. The key motivations for re-branding are given in Table 21.1.

RISKS OF RE-BRANDING

Clearly, there is a risk that any re-branding will lead to a fall in market share. Re-branding offers an opportunity to grow sales – and with it comes the possibility that many customers will be alienated by the change. Larger brands often act as informal 'benchmarks' for consumers – and the removal of these benchmarks may prompt consumers to reappraise their preferences and buying habits, and defect to competitors. Re-branding is not a decision to be taken lightly – it is a major strategic move, and should only be undertaken after a thorough assessment of the likely gains and

Table 21.1   Some common motivations for re-branding

Reason for re-branding	Example
To over-haul the brand, giving it a fresh start	Eurodisney renamed Disneyland Paris after a slow start
To recover from a crisis or scandal	valuJet became Airtran after a plane crash
As part of a de-merger or spin-off	Arthur Anderson de-merged into Anderson and Accenture
As part of a merger or acquisition	Sandoz and Ciba-Geigy merged to form Novartis
To harmonize brands internationally	Marathon was re-branded Snickers in the UK
To rationalize a product portfolio	Unilever re-branded Olivio spread under Bertolli banner
To support a new direction for the business	British Petroleum re-branded BP

losses. When a decision to re-brand is taken, communications often focus on establishing the new brand, and may overlook the effect on existing customers.

RE-BRANDING AS A CHANGE MANAGEMENT TOOL

In 1987 British Airways was privatized. The airline had a terrible reputation in Britain, where people would joke that BA stood for 'Bloody Awful'. It was a stodgy corporation, highly unprofitable, with disaffected employees and a reputation for incompetence. Customer service was, at best, indifferent. The company needed wholesale change.

Responsibility for turning around the ailing airline ultimately rested with the CEO, Sir Colin Marshall. He knew that rapid, widespread change was needed, but realized that this could disorientate both customers and employees. A new, explicit set of values was needed to make sense of the changes – and thus a new brand position was born: 'The World's Favourite Airline.'

Employee satisfaction surveys showed that although morale was low, staff were loyal to the company and really wanted it to succeed. Marshall harnessed this latent goodwill by providing a clear goal: not just to be a successful airline, but to be the favourite among customers – only by providing efficient operations and first-class standards of service could British Airways hope to fulfil this goal.

The clarity of this new brand strategy gave employees a reason to accept some of the sacrifices that come with the comprehensive transformation of a business: extensive downsizing, restructuring of operational and functional areas, new information systems, new performance evaluation measures and so forth. Dozens of separate change programmes were implemented, each clearly orientated around the brand position.

Within five years, British Airways was an unrecognizable company: popular with customers, profitable, highly competitive and respected within the industry.

RE-BRANDING AND CORPORATE CULTURE

In the mid-1990s British Airways undertook one of the most radical re-branding exercises ever attempted by a major corporation. As the company expanded its global reach, the percentage of British passengers declined. Consolidation in the airline industry made it essential to secure an international customer base. The increasing scale of alliances between airlines put pressure on the BA to globalize.

The trouble was, British Airways was a very *British* company – and this presented some problems. In some parts of the world, 'Britishness' was associated with being aloof and slightly bumbling – and then there was the slightly awkward fact that Britain held much of the world under colonial rule less than a century earlier. The company's new CEO, Robert Ayling, decided that re-branding was necessary if BA was to fulfil its global ambitions.

In many ways, this seemed a natural progression of the existing brand position, 'the world's favourite airline'. The change was one of emphasis: whereas previously, the focus had been on 'the world's *favourite* airline', now BA would become 'the *world's* favourite airline'. This apparently small shift had massive effects – the most visible of which was the controversial re-branding of BA's fleet.

Most re-brandings pronounce an organization's new identity by stamping a single, iconic mark on all collateral, together with rigid adherence to style guides and colour palettes. Not for BA: in 1996, the airline unveiled a brand scheme that embraced diversity and emphasized different cultures. Artists from different countries were commissioned to decorate the tail-fins of BA's planes.

The idea of using images of ethnic diversity to establish a corporate identity was seamlessly pushed through the company at all levels,[1] from company reports to TV advertising (Figure 21.1). However, from the outset the re-branding ran into problems. At a launch ceremony attended by Lady Thatcher, the former prime minister took one look at a model plane sporting the new ethnic livery and pronounced it 'awful', covering it with her handkerchief.

The re-branding did not seem to be in line with the airline's key stakeholders. The British conservative establishment was hostile to the new global image – and many of them were BA shareholders or customers.

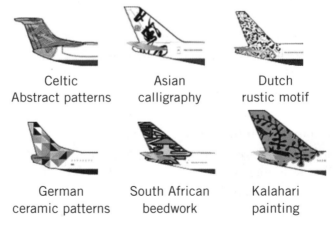

Celtic	Asian	Dutch
Abstract patterns	calligraphy	rustic motif
German	South African	Kalahari
ceramic patterns	beedwork	painting

Figure 21.1 British Airway's bold tail-fin re-branding, featuring ethnic designs

[1] http://www.britishairways.com/lsp/wgallery/wgallery.shtml

Worse than this, the re-branding was not well received by the company's staff. At a time when a fresh round of downsizing was taking place, employees were angered to see the company spending £60 million on its brand, and a strike was organized for the day of the launch.

To add to these difficulties, a rift between the company's culture and its image soon became apparent. On the outside, the brand now appeared to be internationally minded. On the inside, a traditional British culture dominated – polite and prim, with a silver tea service. Despite its boldness and faultless execution, it soon became clear that BA's re-branding was never really going to take off.

In 1998, BA suspended the re-branding, and in 2000, Robert Ayling was replaced as CEO. The tension between the global nature of the airline's customer base and the essential Britishness of the company's culture has still not been fully resolved.

RE-BRANDING AS IMAGE OVERHAUL

Aeroflot was the state airline of the Soviet Union. In 1994 the company was privatized, following the collapse of communism. The airline had a poor safety record, following a series of bizarre incidents – for example, a flight bound for Hong Kong crashed in Siberia after the pilot allowed his 11-year-old daughter and 16-year-old son to take turns on the controls. Aeroflot also suffered a reputation for appalling service. Airline staff dressed in military-style uniforms, and were known for their fearsome manners. The airline became the butt of jokes:

Stewardess: 'Would you like a meal?'
Passenger: 'What are the options?'
Stewardess: 'Yes or No!'

In 2002, some 11 years after the fall of communism, Aeroflot decided that some re-branding might be in order. The growth of the Russian economy had ensured that Aeroflot's revenues had grown, and the airline operated services to 108 destinations in 54 countries. Most importantly, Aeroflot's air safety record improved dramatically: according to the International Civil Aviation Authority, their record is now better than average. The brand has an impressively high awareness across the world – the only problem is that most people still associate Aeroflot with Soviet-era inefficiency.

The airline hired a London-based branding consultancy to refresh the brand. Firstly, the consultancy recommended that the airline keep its name: Aeroflot had a certain fame, and this should be retained. Secondly, they proposed the removal of the 'hammer and sickle' emblem from Aeroflot's logo: if the airline wanted to distance itself from the communist past, this seemed like a good move. Thirdly, the shift away from the 'drab blue', to a more vibrant colour palette was recommended. Fourthly, there was some talk about being 'people focused', and, finally, it was stressed that 'being Russian is part of the brand'.

This re-branding seems to lack the clarity of vision that British Airways found with 'the world's favourite airline': there is little that seems likely to galvanize employees or heighten the interest of customers. To further blunt the purpose of the re-branding, Aeroflot decided that it would retain the hammer and sickle logo (Figure 21.2)[2], after a survey revealed that its removal would be unpopular with staff.

Figure 21.2   *Aeroflot decided to keep the hammer and sickle logo*

[2] Photograph by Suzanne Treister, from 'AEROFLOT Russian Airlines – Global Offices Research Project' 2001 – ongoing Department of Revolutionary Nostalgia, International Corporation of Lost Structures (www.icols.org)

RE-BRANDING TO SUPPORT A NEW DIRECTION

UPS wanted to make it clear that it was no longer purely in the business of express parcel delivery: it is a global logistics company, providing a range of technical and supply chain solutions. The elegant 1961 logo design – with its prominently featured parcel – was no longer appropriate (in any case, for many years UPS have rejected packages with strings because they jam the sorting machines). The new logo is a more masculine shield featuring a swoosh (Figure 21.3), replacing the bow-tied package identity. The launch of the new logo in 2003 was accompanied by extensive communications, establishing the company as a provider of business solutions – not just a mover of packages.

Figure 21.3   UPS *replaced their package logo with a shield*

RE-BRANDING AS COST CONTROL

The re-branding of Northwest Airlines has an unusual motivation. When the company announced its identity switch to NWA, they explained that it was primarily a cost-cutting exercise: the cost of repainting planes would fall by 20%, since the new logo was simpler and required less masking. The re-branding brought additional benefits. Northwest has grown from being a regional US airline into a large global carrier. However, the brand seemed irrelevant to non-American travellers (Northwest of what exactly?), and by re-branding as NWA (Figure 21.4), the airline becomes more accessible to a wider global audience. Presumably Northwest is not concerned about being confused with NWA – Niggaz With Attitude – the unapologetically violent and sexist pioneers

Figure 21.4   *Northwest Airlines re-branded itself NWA*

of gangsta rap. However, it seems that the company didn't quite have the nerve to lose the 'Northwest Airlines' descriptor from the logo.

RE-BRANDING TO CLARIFY CORPORATE STRUCTURE

The Philip Morris brand is synonymous with cigarettes – and has become a focus for much of the controversy surrounding this industry. The company is aware of this, describing the name as 'truly a tobacco name.'[3] However, tobacco has become only one part of the business, which now includes companies such as Kraft, Jacobs and Nabisco. So, in 2003 the company undertook a widespread re-branding and re-structuring. The Philip Morris brand now covers the global tobacco business, while a new brand – Altria – has been launched to cover the parent company.

Altria deny that the re-branding is intended to distance the company from the tobacco business: 'Altria Group takes pride in owning what we believe to be the two premier tobacco companies in the world.' However, many observers are cynical. As a *Forbes* article put it, 'Philip Morris is hoping its new name, Altria, can bleach out the 150-year-old nicotine stains of its cigarette business.'[4] Whether or not this is true, the name change certainly makes clearer the structure of the business, and allows the non-tobacco parts of the company to share the spotlight. As an Altria statement puts it: 'Our new identity will help give stakeholders greater clarity about the structure of our family of companies – about which is the parent and which are the operating companies.' However, a defensive mentality still surrounds the brand: Altria would not, for example, give us permission to show the new logo in this book.

---

[3] http://www.altria.com/about_altria/01_01_corpidenchange.asp
[4] Phoebe Bravakis, 'The rename game', *Forbes*, 24 12 2001.

RE-BRANDING AS A RESPONSE TO CRISIS

If a brand is found to have defrauded investors of some $11 billion, it might reasonably be said to be facing a crisis. This is what happened to the telecommunications company WorldCom, when the scandal broke in 2002 and the senior executives began their long haul through the federal courts. The company managed to survive the subsequent bankruptcy proceedings against it – but the WorldCom brand did not: like Enron before it, WorldCom quickly became a byword for corrupt corporations, as surely as Nixon stands for lying politicians. The company had no choice but to re-brand.

Much of WorldCom's consumer marketing – a smaller, but important part of its business – was done under the MCI brand name. MCI merged with WorldCom in the late 1990s, and dated back to the mid-1960s (Figure 21.5). The MCI brand was reasonably well known and had emerged relatively undamaged by the fraud scandal that engulfed World-Com. The re-branding was essential to the company's recovery, and was a key part of its commitment to creditors and the bankruptcy court. Unsurprisingly, the rhetoric of MCI places heavy emphasis on corporate integrity. Having caused serious speculation about the possible failure of capitalism, MCI now intends to set new standards in stringency and transparency, aiming to 'be a role model for corporate governance.'[5] If this becomes more than rhetoric, it will be a heroic turnaround, and one that will earn the company much genuine respect.

The company was understandably eager to ditch the WorldCom name and declare a fresh start under the MCI brand. However, the transition may have been too fast: as the re-branding happened the company was

Figure 21.5   *WorldCom re-branded itself MCI*

---

[5] http://global.mci.com/values/

still absorbing after-shocks from the scandal. Instead of smudging the name of WorldCom, negative news stories were written about 'MCI, formerly known as WorldCom'. Consequently, the MCI brand has not escaped taint – which may fade with time, but could have been avoided if the company had delayed the re-branding until the dust had completely settled.

22

Acquire

Increasingly, the focus of acquisitions is not the company's offices or factories, or its machinery – but the *brand*. Tangible brick-and-mortar assets are often only of secondary interest to a prospective buyer. Often, the real value lies in the possibilities presented by taking ownership of a new brand. As a United Biscuits chief once said (put into poem form by Paul Feldwick[1]):

> Buildings age and become dilapidated.
> Machines wear out.
> People die.
> But what live on are the brands.

This explains the increase in the amounts that companies are prepared to pay to acquire brands – financial analysts have recognized the long-term value that may be locked in a brand. Until the 1980s, the price of an acquisition was determined solely by the financial performance of the target company – typically, around eight to 10 times the company's profits. This was shattered by a series of exuberant acquisitions: Groupe Danone paid $2.5 billion for Nabisco Europe – at a price:earning ratio of 27. This was followed by Nestlé, which bought Rowntree Macintosh at a ratio of 26. Times had changed: it's now common for companies to pay more to acquire strong brands, and ratios are frequently around 20.

---

[1] Quoted by Paul Feldwick in his book *What is Brand Equity, Anyway?* WARC.

REASONS FOR ACQUIRING A BRAND

There are many reasons a company may acquire a new brand. For example, a company may seek to create value from existing operations: Energizer bought Schick-Wilkinson Sword because it could use the same salesforce to push both batteries and shaving products through the same distribution channels. This strategy – known as *deriving synergies* – was also used by Gillette, which bought Duracell batteries. The reasons for acquisition are numerous. Some of the key motivations for acquiring a new brand are given in Table 22.1.

ACQUIRE TO ENTER NEW MARKETS

Traditionally, if a company wanted to enter a new market, then it would buy an appropriate manufacturer with a reliable, efficient, factory operation. Today, companies are mainly interested in buying a place in people's heads – not buying manufacturing plants. Recent years have seen many operational elements become highly streamlined – the route to real competitive advantage often lies within the strength of a brand.

Table 22.1   Key reasons for acquiring a brand

Reason for acquisition	Example
To enter new markets	LVMH buys prestige watch brands Ebel, Chaumet and TAG Heuer
To unlock latent brand value	The Himmel Group buys Ovaltine
To derive synergies	Energizer buys Schick-Wilkinson Sword to gain distribution synergies
To buy the competition	Online trading firm Ameritrade buys TradeCast and Datek
To complete a portfolio of brands	Ford buys Jaguar and Landrover
To adapt to a changing market	WD-40 buys 3-IN-ONE, Lava, Carpet Fresh and Solvol
As a re-branding exercise	Roxio buys Napster in order to use the brand name

In 1998, when BMW wanted to enter the high-end luxury car market, it bought the right to use the Rolls Royce brand name and its associated symbols. BMW avoided buying the ageing Rolls Royce factories, paying £40 million just to use the famous name. Many commentators thought this valuation 'on the cheap'[2] and, in any case, Rolls Royce subsequently lent the £40 million back to BMW in order to build new factories in Britain to build new Rolls Royce models.

ACQUIRE TO UNLOCK LATENT VALUE

Brand strength is of course no guarantee of success: a brand may have high levels of awareness and a strong heritage but nonetheless be drifting into decline. Its owners may lack the vision or resources to capitalize on the strength of the brand – or it may simply be neglected as a 'non-core' part of the business. In some cases, the owners may recognize that the best way to reap value from the brand is to sell it, and focus on core brands.

- In 2003 Pfizer Inc. sold a number of confectionery brands to Cadbury Schweppes Plc – including Chiclets, Trident, Dentyne, Bubblicious, Halls and Clorets. Cadbury is convinced that it can more effectively market these brands, as well as deriving $185 million in cost synergies.
- In 1991 the Himmel Group – a business which exists to turn around 'orphan brands' – bought the neglected Gold Bond talcum powder brand. Through brand extension and advertising, they grew sales from $1 million in 1991 to $27 million in 1995.
- Rather than completely sell off the brands Complan and Castilian, Heinz decided that a joint venture with Saatchinvest was the best option. Saatchinvest was formed to acquire 'under-utilized' brands, with the help of advertising agency M&C Saatchi.

Major brand owners are increasingly quick to rationalize their portfolios: and the pickings may be rich for entrepreneurial businesses such as

---

[2] *Financial Times* 'Lex' column, quoted in Tony Tollington, *Brand Assets*. John Wiley & Sons, 2002.

Himmel Group and Saatchinvest, which are well placed to profit from unlocking latent brand value. Himmel has used some simple but apparently effective tactics for turning around dormant brands:

- *Bare-bones ads.* Basic, cheap and succinct ads emphasizing the brand name and product benefits.
- *Airwaves blitz.* Simultaneous play of a number of different TV and radio spots.
- *Product extensions.* Rapidly follow airwave blitz with new products to catch consumers' attention and extend opportunities for sales.

This simple formula has yielded impressive results for the Himmel Group's brands. In 1992 Himmel bought the famous Ovaltine malted drink and immediately launched a revitalization campaign. Retail sales doubled within the first 100 days of the campaign – and this success proved to be sustainable: Ovaltine commanded 29% of the mixed chocolate drinks market in 2001, up from 11% in 1992.

ACQUIRE TO ADAPT TO CHANGE

Acquiring a new brand can transform a company, allowing it to adapt to changing market conditions. In many companies, 'Research & Development' has become eclipsed by 'Acquisition & Development': it's often cheaper, faster and less risky to buy an emerging brand than to develop it from scratch.

WD-40 is the highly recognized brand name of a highly successful product – a multi-purpose, petroleum-based lubricant. The company was a cash cow, generating $830000 per employee in 2000 – investors had become used to generous dividends. However, by the mid-1990s it was becoming clear that market conditions were changing. Two trends in particular threatened the continued success of the WD-40 brand:

- Consolidation of retailers meant greater buyer power: fewer and larger customers were pressurizing profit margins.
- Demand for WD-40 was flat – the market was saturated (a can of WD-40 can last a long time).

A new management team was installed, led by CEO Garry Ridge. He persuaded shareholders to adopt a strategy that would maximize the long-term value of the company. Ridge's strategy cast WD-40 as a 'fortress brand', and set out to transform the company into a 'fortress of brands': 'Each brand must complement the others, creating a whole that is greater than the sum of its parts.'[3]

So, WD-40 suspended its generous dividend payments, and instead went on an acquisition spending spree – guided by a simple identity statement: 'We live under the sinks, in the garages and in the toolboxes of the world.' The acquisitions included 3-IN-ONE Oil, Lava heavy-duty soap, X14 stain removers and Carpet Fresh rug deodorizers.

Apart from generating at least £70 million in additional annual sales, the new range of WD-40 brands give it added strength when negotiating with retail buyers – enabling it to defend margins. In the company's first post-acquisition year of trading, profits were up 20.3%, and stock value has increased from about $18 a share in 2000 to around $33 in Q4 2003.

BRANDS ARE NOT ALWAYS SEPARABLE ASSETS

To buy or sell a brand asset, it must be 'detachable' from the rest of the company – the people, the premises, technologies and products. Accountants call this 'separability', and there is plenty of debate about whether brands can really be separated from the context that created them. In many respects, the idea of a complex organization like IBM selling its name to another company is no less absurd than the thought of Woody Allen selling his name to Donald Rumsfeld. Some brands – like people's names – become an inherent part the organization, and vice versa.

The difficulty lies in the nature of brands: they live in people's head, not on companies' books. They are the result of people's experiences and associations. A brand is therefore the consequence of the behaviours of an organization – remove a brand from its context, and it becomes a

---

[3] Quoted in P.L. Currie and T.G. Malott, 'Reinvention through acquisition: How WD-40 dealt its way to strategic long-term value', M&A Today, July 2002.

different brand. In an essay entitled 'Giving up the ghost in the machine', Stagliano and O'Malley suggest that we conceive of brands 'as actions, not artifacts; as enactments, not espousals; as behaviours not essences; in a word, as machines without ghosts'.[4]

Under this view, brands are not always conveniently detachable assets that can be easily bought and sold – they're an intrinsic part of the company. In the light of this, we give some comparisons which serve to illustrate some of the potential 'do and don't' of acquiring a brand.

DO-AND-DON'T #1: V2 MUSIC VS BENETTON

When Richard Branson sold his Virgin record label to EMI for $800 million, part of the deal was that he would stay out of the music industry for at least four years. When this restriction expired, Branson was ready with a strategy to create a new major music label – and in November 1996 V2 Music was launched. Branson's plan has two key elements.

1. **Rapid growth through acquisition.** He set up a fighting fund of some $300 million and went on a shopping spree, buying up a number of small independent labels – such as New York's Gee Street Records. Almost instantly, V2 Music had a stable of successful artists, such as the Jungle Brothers, Moby and the Stereophonics.
2. **Creative autonomy of the 'sublabels'.** Branson realized that independent labels are often the product of – and focus of – their cultural context. Real music fans are passionate and highly committed to 'their' style of music: they feel part of a movement. The artists are an integral part of all this. To keep them at their creative peak, Branson's strategy was to keep them close to their roots, and thus allow the greatest possible artistic freedom to the labels acquired by V2.

By pursuing this strategy, Branson was able to build a record label which combined the creative energy of an independent with the marketing and

---

[4] A. Stagliano and D. O'Malley, 'Giving up the ghost in the machine', in M. Earls and M. Baskin (eds), *Brand New Brand Thinking*, Kogam Page, 2002.

distribution muscle of a major. V2 Music took opportunities to derive syn-ergies between labels wherever possible – but maintaining independence for the sublabels was always paramount.

Branson's approach stands in contrast with that taken by Benetton, which became known as 'the brand killer'[5] – such was the company's ability to put market-leading brands into intensive care. In the 1990s, Benetton bought a number of sporting goods brands – at a reported cost of nearly $900. These included Nordica ski boots, Nordica skis (originally Kästle), Rollerblade and Prince Tennis.

The theory was that these brands would benefit from Benetton's appar-ent retail expertise, while driving sales of Benetton's core products (cus-tomers buying ski boots might be tempted to buy some brightly coloured chunky knitwear). The reality was very different: for each of the acquired brands, market shares shrank. What went wrong?

Unlike V2 Music, Benetton sought to integrate its new brands as much as possible. They would share a salesforce, administration staff and offices, and even a marketing department. This aggressive centralization was strictly implemented, and the result was to tip the brands into a long-term nosedive: both Nordica and Prince, for example, slipped from market leaders to number three.

By 2001 Benetton realized a change of approach was needed, and brought in George Napier as CEO. His assessment of the troubled sports brands was clear: 'The people who are in these businesses are often in them because they love that activity. If you sap that, you have nothing – internally or competitively.'[6]

This can be seen most clearly in the case of Rollerblade, which was bought by Benetton in 1998. The company has grown up in a part of Min-nesota which is described as 'skating mad'. At lunchtimes, employees held roller-hockey tournaments. The success of the company was fuelled by the genuine enthusiasm of its people: they loved rollerblading, and were proud to work for Rollerblade. In many respects, they *were* Rollerblade.

This was Benetton's mistake: of Rollerblade's 80 employees, 59 were fired and the remaining 21 were invited to move to an office complex 1000 miles southeast. All made the move – and all but one had returned

---

[5] Paul Hochman, 'The brand killer', FSB: *Fortune Small Business*, May 2002.
[6] See footnote 5.

to Minnesota within a year. Effectively, the brand's core had been dismantled. Benetton owned the name and the products, but had lost the passion and vision of the employees.

Rollerblade lost sales volume – indeed, sales collapsed across the entire category. The other acquired sports brands suffered from similar treatment. It's a dramatic example of the inseparability of brands – they are embodied in the context that created them. As the Benetton case shows, this is more than an accounting technicality or a philosophical conjecture – it has substantial consequences for brand management.

DO-AND-DON'T #2: SNAPPLE

The lessons learned from comparing the approaches of V2 Music and Benetton are brought to life vividly in a *Harvard Business Review* article about the case of Snapple. John Deighton, the article's author, reaches the following conclusion:

> There is a vital interplay between the challenges a brand faces and the culture of the corporation that owns it. When brand and culture fall out of alignment, both brand and corporate owner are likely to suffer.[7]

This clearly describes the poor performance of Rollerblade after the acquisition by Benetton, and the case of Snapple provides some similar lessons. Snapple had two owners between 1993 and 2000: Quaker Oats and Triarc Beverages. The performance of the brand under these two custodians could not be more different:

- Quaker Oats bought Snapple for $1.7 billion in 1993 and sold it to Triarc Beverages in 1997 for $300 million – a phenomenal collapse of brand value.
- Triarc Beverages turned the brand around astonishingly quickly, selling it to Cadbury's Schweppes for $1 billion in 2000.

---

[7] John Deighton, 'How Snapple got its juice back' *Harvard Business Review*, January 2002.

What happened? The explanation starts with the Snapple brand itself, which had grown up on the streets of New York in the 1970s. Snapple was a cheeky upstart apple-juice brand which won over New Yorkers – and soon the rest of the US – with its effortless mix of home-made fresh-ness and endearing amateurism. The advertising and packaging seemed home-made and amateurish, and the spokesperson for the brand was the order-processing clerk called Wendy, a true Noo Yawker who came to be affectionately known as the Snapple Lady. Against the slick marketing of other beverages, this down-to-earth naturalness stood out a mile. As Deighton puts it, 'Some brands just want to have fun, and from birth Snapple was one of them.'[8]

When Quaker Oats bought Snapple in 1993, the brand's success was a matter of corporate survival. The company had one very successful beverage brand – Gatorade – but was vulnerable to larger players that had broader portfolios (in the end, Quaker fell prey to take-over, and is now a part of Pepsi Co.). The stakes were high, and consequently Quaker's marketing plan for Snapple was focused on minimizing risk.

Quaker applied the textbook marketing approaches that they had used successfully with Gatorade: rationalizing distribution channels, rational-izing product lines, looking for synergies with existing brands, and exten-sive brand awareness campaigns. However, some of these textbook measures didn't suit the Snapple brand. For example, Quaker launched larger bottle sizes: they understood that larger 32- and 64-ounce bottles were more profitable, but didn't realize that Snapple's lunchtime con-sumers just aren't that thirsty.

Quaker also understood that to achieve large volumes, Snapple had to appeal to a mainstream consumer base – and assumed that to do this, the advertising had to be mainstream. Perhaps Quaker's executives misun-derstood the appeal of Snapple's early advertising, and eagerly spotted an opportunity to inject some slick production values. In any case, in all areas Snapple's quirky amateurism was replaced by mainstream blandness. Finally, they sacked Wendy, the much-loved Snapple Lady.

The subsequent failure of the brand led to its sale to Triarc Beverages, which is described as 'the sort of place where employees wear

---

[8] See footnote 7.

costumes to work on Halloween.'[9] The Triarc team took up the challenge with great relish: 'We started loving the brand from the first day', says CEO marketing director Ken Gilbert. 'I don't think there was anyone at Quaker who had loved that brand.'

Triarc began by reversing some of the more obviously damaging decisions that had been taken by Quaker. They withdrew the unpopular big bottles, and reintroduced Wendy by wrapping her picture on the bottle. Most importantly, their attitude was true to the roots of the brand: for example, whereas Quaker's approach to product development was risk minimization, Triarc said 'give-it-a-go!'. With low development costs, new products were launched all the time – the marketplace was a space for experimentation. This inspired employees, who could see their ideas come to light. As one put it, 'We drank the ideas.'

As we said earlier, in many ways brands are behaviours – they are actions, not assets. In his *Harvard Business Review* article, John Deighton offers a perspective on this theme:

> Brand meanings and associations arise as a kind of found consensus between what the marketer wants and what the consumer has use for. Precisely because they were planned with a professional thoroughness and care foreign to the brand, Quaker's moves with Snapple shattered that consensus. Triarc's gleeful experimentation restored it.

---

[9] See footnote 7.

PART IV
Brand Biographies

In Part II (Sources of Business Value) we saw the many ways that brands can create value for business – from attracting and retaining talent, to stimulating new product development. We described how a brand can play a role as a management tool, enhancing business performance in critical areas. In Part III (Strategic Brand Planning) we looked at the challenges that face brands as they grow, and at some approaches for dealing with market changes. In this section we pull these themes together by looking at 'biographies' of seven well-known brands.

- For **American Express**, the brand's premium status is at the heart of the company's business model. Established in 1850, this brand certainly has some lessons on sustaining a brand over the long term.
- For **Ben & Jerry's**, their *values-led* approach to business is embodied in their brand. Employees, customers and suppliers all respond to the company's values: great ice-cream, down-to-earth attitudes, social and environmental activism – and all with a sense of fun.
- For **Def Jam**, it's all about keeping a real connection with music fans. The brand embodies this relationship – it's 'a lifestyle brand that happens to sell music'. Not only has this enabled the company to weather the storms hitting the music industry, but Def Jam has also been expanding into new areas.
- For **IBM**, revitalizing the brand was crucial to driving the company's famous turnaround. The brand was key: structural and operational improvements would amount to nothing unless the company's culture embraced them. For IBM, the brand was the starting point for change.
- For **Dove**, the strength of the brand has fuelled phenomenal growth. The Dove brand has played a dual role, providing options for

extensions into new country markets, and for extension into new product areas.

- For **BP**, the brand is a unifying force across the company's huge, diverse global operations. The BP brand communicates a clear purpose to employees, investors, governments, pressure groups, customers and suppliers: BP's brand strategy and its corporate strategy aren't separate.
- For *The Economist*, investing in the brand – as opposed to merely advertising next week's content – has yielded impressive results: apart from a massive increase in circulation and an increase in its advertising rate card, *The Economist* has expanded into new business areas.

Each of these is discussed in detail, and the contribution of the brand is clearly outlined. We begin by describing the heritage of the brand, before looking at its role within the company's overall business model. Finally, an overview of the company's financial performance is given.

23

American Express

While there are many directions a financial services company can go today, we will only do that which supports the growth of our brand.

Ken Chenault, CEO

BACKGROUND

American Express issues more charge cards and credit cards than any other company. It's also the world's largest travel agent, and a well-respected global financial services provider. The American Express brand is regarded as one of the world's most powerful brands – ranked 15th in Interbrand's Global Brand Scorecard, and also in Corebrand's 2002 Corporate Branding Index. As we shall see, brand strategy is integral to American Express's operations.

HERITAGE

Founded in 1850, American Express is one of the world's oldest brands, and its history contains some interesting lessons on how to sustain a brand over the long term. The company originally offered freight express services, and people began to trust the company to provide secure delivery of their valuables across the frontier. The express wagon riders became idolized as rugged, determined individuals, and the American Express brand came to stand for exemplary customer service.

During the late nineteenth century, Americans developed a rapacious appetite for European travel, and American Express expanded its freight services to Europe. Americans abroad came to rely upon the company for travel advice, and the overseas offices became informal consulates – a 'home away from home'. Increasingly, the company became a travel services business – and this was consolidated in 1891 with the invention of travellers' cheques.

A turning point came with the outbreak of World War I. More than 150000 Americans were left stranded in Europe, many of whom were without funds or access to funds, and without any way to get themselves or their belongings back home. Across Europe, lines formed outside American Express offices (Figure 23.1). As a Rotterdam office manager wrote: 'Our entire front hall was packed to capacity with people who had completely lost their heads, their money, or their belongings.'

Remarkably, American Express had anticipated a crisis, and had built up large reserves of cash and foreign currency. The company negotiated safe passage with railway companies and ocean liners, and even reunited

Figure **23.1** *In 1914, war-stranded Americans across Europe turned to American Express for help*

15000 abandoned pieces of luggage with their rightful owners. During this crisis, the company earned considerable gratitude and goodwill, and a lasting reputation for delivering a reliable, first-class service for travellers.

BRAND STRATEGY

American Express has carefully nurtured its reputation as a dependable financial stalwart with brand positions such as 'As good as gold around the world' and 'Don't leave home without it' (Figure 23.2). Unlike many competitors – for example, Visa – American Express is cautious of affinity marketing strategies because of the risk to the brand. Affinity arrangements make it possible to issue cards to the customers of partners, thereby reducing the costs of acquiring and managing card members. However, for American Express, high standards of customer service are essential to maintaining the brand's premium status, and the risk of jeopardizing this is considered too great.

As a global company with a well-travelled clientele, American Express needs a strong, well-managed worldwide brand. To deliver this, the company has partnered with a global advertising network – Ogilvy & Mather – with whom it has been working since 1962. American

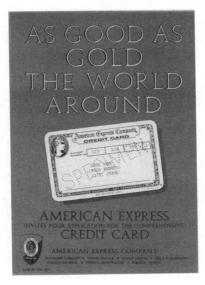

Figure 23.2   *A 1958 print ad for American Express*

Express has recently undertaken a repositioning of the brand in order to shake-off some associations with the flashy, conspicuous consumption of the 1980s. American Express views its customers as people whose aspirations are broader than material acquisition, but who want to experience the best that life has to offer. The 'Long Live Dreams' brand positioning was developed in order to recognize this, and the 'Make Life Rewarding' campaign, launched in March 2002, outlined the specific benefits American Express can deliver (including an extensive rewards programme).

THE ROLE OF THE BRAND

For American Express, the brand is more than a marketing tool or a corporate identity – it's an essential element of the long-term business model. American Express describes the role of the brand in terms of a 'Virtuous Circle', which is illustrated in Figure 23.3. Long-standing investment in the brand has developed strong associations with quality, service and success. This premium brand position attracts customers who are likely to spend more than customers of other cards. Of course, big spenders are attractive to merchants, and American Express is able to make a higher charge – discount rate – in exchange for high-value customers.

The brand is a crucial step in this virtuous circle: American Express is able to reinvest revenues from their higher discount rate into maintain-

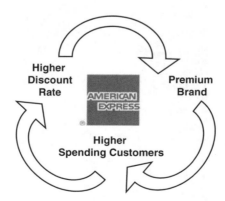

Figure 23.3 *The Virtuous Circle in American Express's card business (source: American Express)*

ing high-quality standards of service, into an extensive rewards programme, and into brand communications and advertising.

This central role of the brand can be seen in the company's three operating principles:

1. Provide value for customers
2. Achieve best-in-class economics
3. Ensure that all actions enhance the value of the brand.

Consequently, the brand is a crucial component of American Express's operations. Recent years have seen a number of activities aimed at further strengthening the brand and promoting its role within the company. The results of this are evident in employee satisfaction surveys: in 2002, 83% of employees said that they felt encouraged to take the brand into account when making decisions – an increase from 75% in 2000. This level of confidence and commitment to the brand is essential if American Express is to deliver first-class standards of service.

FINANCIAL PERFORMANCE

American Express has placed its brand at the heart of the corporate strategy – and this should be reflected in its financial results. Most analysts agree that the brand strength has helped the company to sustain higher returns than other financial services companies. A report on American Express by the investment bank Bear Stearns gives a comparison of returns on equity (Figure 23.4).

The comparison shows that American Express's return on equity is 5–6% higher than the industry average. This is taken to be a common result for companies that have strong brands: Bear Sterns cite a report by McKinsey, which shows that returns for such companies are consistently 2–5% higher than for industry counterparts. The analysts conclude their report into the strength of the American Express brand as follows:

> By investing heavily in its brand, we believe American Express can sustain higher returns for a longer period than most of its competitors. We believe the company's ability to maintain its brand has

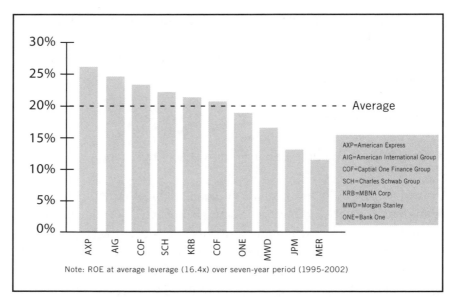

Figure 23.4   *Return on equity comparison*

enabled it to differentiate itself not only in the card business, but also in its travel business and, eventually, in its asset management business. American Express brand (reputation, products, value, service, experience) has enabled it to profitably acquire business partners and customers . . . despite intense competition.[1]

---

[1] Bear Sterns, 'American Express Co. The Power of the Brand', September 2003.

24

Ben & Jerry's

Two regular, caring guys living in Vermont, the land of the cows and green pastures, making some world class ice-cream in some pretty unusual flavors.

Ben & Jerry's positioning statement[1]

BACKGROUND

Ben & Jerry's is a global ice-cream brand with annual sales in the region of €1.5 billion. Owned by Unilever since 2000, Ben & Jerry's produces 'superpremium' ice-cream – high fat content with low aeration, resulting in a richer, creamier taste – competing with brands such as Haagen-Dazs from Diageo. The range of ice-cream is made using natural ingredients, and includes some unconventional flavours – such as Phish Food and Chunky Monkey. The brand is well known for its commitment to social and environmental causes, and contributes 7.5% of pre-tax profits to philanthropic causes. Ben & Jerry's has successfully managed two major transitions: firstly, from a local start-up to a national brand with widespread distribution, and, secondly, from an independent, founder-run business to a part of a large multinational corporation.

---

[1] Ben Cohen and Jerry Greenfield, 'Ben & Jerry's Double Dip', *Fireside*, 1997.

HERITAGE

Ben Cohen and Jerry Greenfield did not set out to build a successful business, let alone one of the world's most famous ice-cream brands. In 1977, when the two old high-school friends decided to split the cost of a $5 ice-cream-making correspondence course, they were merely looking for a way to earn a living – one that didn't involve working for someone else, and preferably one that involved food.

From the outset, Ben & Jerry's was an unconventional company. Setting up an ice-cream parlour in Burlington, Vermont – a place known for its long, cold winters and short summers – doesn't seem like an act of great business acumen. From the founders' point of view, however, this meant that at least there were no competitors. Moreover, Burlington had a large student population, and students – in Ben and Jerry's experience – eat a lot of ice-cream.

Armed with a four-gallon freezer and based in an old gas station, Ben and Jerry went into business. Intent on making high-quality ice-cream, their reputation among the locals soon spread – and they were selling all the ice-cream they could make. Added to this, the founders themselves became much loved – always pulling stunts and throwing free ice-cream parties. They printed up some bumper stickers, and soon cars across Burlington were displaying 'Ben & Jerry's' stickers.

People loved the product and responded to the down-to-earth sense of fun of the founders. These were not over-eager entrepreneurs keen to make their fortune – they were two 'regular guys' trying to earn a living and enjoying themselves in the process. 'People wanted us to succeed,' says Jerry. 'They wanted to help these two real guys who obviously needed a lot of help!' explains Ben.[2]

A formative moment for the Ben & Jerry's brand came in 1982, when the company received an acquisition offer. By this time, Ben & Jerry's had become a substantial small business, distributed through supermarkets and opening new stores. The founders didn't like the idea of becoming 'real business people running a real business' and decided to sell up and move on. However, their experience with potential buyers was negative – their

---

[2] See footnote 1.

exposure to corporate wheeler-dealing provoked some real soul searching. Ben visited his old, eccentric mentor Maurice Purpora to seek advice:

> I said, 'Maurice, you know what business does. It exploits the community, it exploits employees, it exploits the environment.' Maurice said 'Ben, you own the company. If there's something you don't like about the way business is done, why don't you just do it different?' That had never occurred to me before.[3]

This was a watershed for Ben & Jerry's: the founders had nearly sold their business, but instead had refocused their priorities – both as individuals and for their company. Now they could articulate a purpose – which they described not with a grand imperative mission statement, but as an *experiment*: 'To see whether a business can survive whilst being a force for progressive social change.'

Thus all the elements of the Ben & Jerry's brand were in place: a high-quality product ('great tasting ice-cream'), unusual flavours, an experimental attitude, a sense of fun, and social and environmental activism – all encompassed by the personalities of Ben Cohen and Jerry Greenfield.

BRAND STRATEGY

Most premium ice-cream brands have sophisticated, foreign-sounding names such as Haagen-Dazs, La Glace de Paris, Alpen Zauber and Frusen Glädjē – although most of these are owned, manufactured and consumed entirely in the US. It's easy to see why Ben & Jerry's stands out from the crowd – the brand's down-home authenticity stands in contrast to the pretensions of its competitors. This is the cornerstone of branding for Ben & Jerry's: *be real*.

Ben & Jerry's has long eschewed traditional packaged goods approaches to branding, which the founders regarded as attempts to falsely associate products with desirable qualities – sexiness, coolness, power. Not only is this essentially dishonest, in the view of the founders, but it is done using

---

[3] See footnote 1.

techniques which themselves have no real value to society. Conventional branding, they believed,

> consists of throwing billions of dollars and tremendous human resources at creating what often amounts to fairy tales that are of no intrinsic value, outside of possible entertainment, to anyone.[4]

Instead, Ben & Jerry's prefer a more organic approach to building a brand: word of mouth, fuelled by 'a great product, a fun, caring environment, and community involvement'. In this sense, all activities are branding activities, and the whole company has a marketing function. Where Ben & Jerry's do distinct marketing activities, they focus their efforts in areas that can add value in some way to people's lives, as the following examples show:

- Regular outdoor festivals with typical attendance of around 40000 people, featuring free live music, stands for non-profit organizations, and plenty of free food (particularly ice-cream).
- Solar-powered sample-buses with portable music-stage, dancers, and plenty of free ice-cream – gives away information about alternative energy sources as well as bringing people to the brand.
- Promoting social causes on packaging – e.g. encouraging consumers to write to their congressman to complain about underfunding of Head Start, a programme to tackle delinquency. As well as promoting an idea, campaigns such as this create powerful brand differentiation.
- Launching a new product line by throwing ice cream parties across the US in honour of individuals working for social change – such as a Chicago high school girl who was campaigning against local gangs. As well as promoting a social message, these were highly effective sampling events which created much local media interest.

These are examples of the non-conventional approaches that Ben & Jerry's used to build the brand, using communications that had some intrinsic social value. However, the most important element in the Ben

---

[4] See footnote 1.

& Jerry's brand has always been great tasting ice-cream. In the last example, although people loved the launch parties, the product was a dismal failure: people tried it, but they didn't like it.

THE ROLE OF THE BRAND

In pursuit of the company's great experiment – to see whether a business could be both successful and contribute towards social progress – Ben & Jerry's adopted a 'values-led' approach to business. These values would be at the heart of the brand – they would *be* the brand. These values are articulated as three missions, described in Table 24.1.[5]

Ben & Jerry's value-led brand is at the heart of the company's operations, and guides decision-making at every level of the organization.

Table 24.1　Ben & Jerry's 'value-led' brand

Product Mission	To make, distribute and sell the finest quality all natural ice-cream and euphoric concoctions with a continued commitment to incorporating wholesome, natural ingredients and promoting business practices that respect the Earth and the Environment.
Economic Mission	To operate the company on a sustainable financial basis of profitable growth, increasing value for our stakeholders and expanding opportunities for development and career growth for our employees.
Social Mission	To operate the company in a way that actively recognizes the central role that business plays in society by initiating innovative ways to improve the quality of life locally, nationally and internationally.

---

[5] www.benjerry.com

By providing a unifying direction for the company, the brand's values generate synergies within the business by bringing together different activities. One example is the creation of the successful *Rainforest Crunch* flavour.

Ben & Jerry's regard their influence as a buyer as an opportunity to promote progressive social change. *Rainforest Crunch* came about as a result of Ben Cohen's interest in sustainable rainforest development – finding rainforest crops that can be equally profitable when harvested clearing the forest for timber. One crop which was potentially sustainable *and* profitable was Brazil nuts. In order to stimulate demand for Brazil nuts, Ben & Jerry's developed a new product which would use them as an ingredient – and *Rainforest Crunch* was born. The packaging of the *Rainforest Crunch* pint explained the background of the product. The ice-cream was an instant success, and was soon a top-selling flavour, generating much publicity.

Ben & Jerry's was able to achieve several objectives by being led by its brand values: sourcing, NPD and marketing. *Rainforest Crunch* was a highly successful flavour which further helped to differentiate the Ben & Jerry's brand.

The focus on its brand values has allowed Ben & Jerry's to attract talented and motivated employees. A number of academic studies and surveys have been conducted among Ben & Jerry's employees, and all conclude that staff feel an extra level of commitment towards the organization because of its social mission. Here are some verbatims:

- *'If I worked for a company without those values it would be a lot less motivating.'*
- *'With my background, I wouldn't have come to work for Ben & Jerry's except this is fun for me.'*
- *'I worked at a Fortune 500 company for years. What attracted me to Ben & Jerry's was that I believe in what Ben & Jerry's believes in.'*

Some people even report having their own perspectives on business changed by working at Ben & Jerry's:

- *'There's been a huge shift in my values and in what makes me feel I'm being effective today.'*

Figure 24.1 *Ben & Jerry's operations interlock around a 'value-led' brand*

Ben & Jerry's finances are also driven by brand values (Figure 24.1). In order to instill a spirit of fairness and teamwork, the company enforced an income ratio between the top and bottom earners, so that the disparity would be limited. When the company first issued shares, the flotation was limited to residents of Vermont – ensuring that the company was fully embodied in (and supported by) the local community. In order to drive the social mission through profits, the Ben & Jerry's Foundation was established.

Ben & Jerry's Director of Materials, Debra Heintz-Parente, described the central role of the brand values in the following way:

> What we're trying to do here is very holistic. The whole company has to believe in the mission, be integrated on the vision and on using it to leverage the company. When it's for real, the suppliers know it, the employees know it, and the customers know it. You can't buy the kind of loyalty that creates.

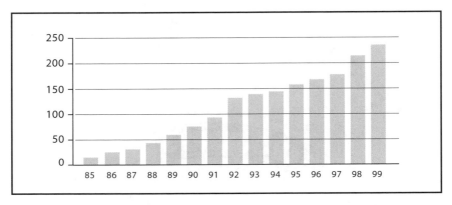

Figure 24.2   *Ben & Jerry's revenue growth 1985–1999 ($m)* (combined source: Ben & Jerry's annual reports)

FINANCIAL PERFORMANCE

Ben & Jerry's has shown steady growth throughout its history, as illustrated in Figure 24.2. Twenty-three years after the business began in a fixed-up gas station in Vermont, it was acquired by Unilever for $326 million in 2000. At the time of acquisition, Ben & Jerry's sales were $237 million, with profits of $13.5 million – that's a price to sales revenue ratio of 1.37. By 2003 annual sales were estimated by Unilever to be within the region of €1.5 billion – at the same price:revenue ratio of 1.37 that gives the Ben & Jerry's brand an estimated value of €2.05 billion.

Looking to the future, it will be interesting to see if this success impacts Ben & Jerry's values-led approach to business. Already, some of the early tenets have been abandoned. The salary ratio, for example, had to be scrapped: the company needed higher calibre senior executives to manage a worldwide expansion and could not compete at the top salary end, while at the bottom end wages were becoming disproportionately high. Ben & Jerry's is now operating at a large global scale, and continuing to be true to its original brand values will require more commitment than ever.

25

Def Jam

> *I've always said Def Jam is a lifestyle company that happens to sell music*
> Lyor Cohen

BACKGROUND

Def Jam is a highly successful music label, described by Forbes as 'probably the most powerful black music label since Motown'.[1] Def Jam launched many of the original rap icons, such as Public Enemy, LL Cool J and the Beastie Boys. Today, the label is home to top-selling stars Jay-Z, Ja Rule and DMX.

In 1999, Def Jam was merged with Island Records to form the Island Def Jam Music Group, a division of Vivendi Universal's Universal Music Group – which itself is the world's biggest music company. In an industry struggling to adapt to changes in technology, Def Jam has continued to grow revenues, and as competitors cut back their operations, Def Jam has expanded into new markets.

HERITAGE

Def Jam is known as the label that pioneered hip hop – a style of music which now generates over $5 billion in worldwide music sales each year.

---

[1] Melanie Wells and Peter Kafka, 'Deft Jams', *Forbes*, 2/4/2002, Vol. 169, Issue 3.

From its origins on the streets of New York, hip hop has become a mainstream industry: in 2000, hip hop accounted for nearly 13% of the $14.3 billion US music market – second only to good old fashioned rock (24%). As a cultural and commercial force, hip hop's impact is formidable: Coke, Pepsi, Gucci, Bacardi, Burberry, Mercedes, Nike and McDonald's are among the many brands that have used hip hop to sell themselves. According to *Business Week*, 'marketing experts estimate that one-quarter of all discretionary spending in America today is influenced by hip hop'.[2]

It was not ever thus. When Def Jam was founded in 1984, hip hop couldn't even get radio play. The major record labels didn't take the emerging style seriously, dismissing it as a fad. Def Jam was to change all that. Def Jam founder Russell Simmons became aware of rap while studying sociology in Harlem. He would watch crowds gather in parks and on street corners to listen to rappers taking turns to perform. Inspired by the enthusiasm of the crowd, Simmons recognized the vast potential of the music. He left college and began promoting rap club nights, going on to form the Def Jam record label when he met an aspiring rap producer, Rick Rubin.

In these early days Def Jam acted as a catalyst for hip hop: finding and developing artists and establishing an audience – and through this, building a business. For Simmons, this was bigger than business – although there's no doubting his commercial acumen. He could see that hip hop was booming because it provided young inner-city blacks with a sense of self-respect. As one commentator described it:

> [hip hop] romanticized the dangerous, exiting characters of the street . . . made poverty and powerlessness into strength by making rappers superhuman, indomitable. The audience followed, finding power in dancing and dressing styles of the moment; in mimicking the swaggering, tougher-than-leather attitude; and by worshiping their street 'poets'.[3]

Def Jam's role in promoting this movement earned it a genuine respect and credibility, much of which survives to this day. Few labels at the time

---

[2] Susan Berfield, Diane Brady and Tom Lowry, 'The CEO of Hip Hop', *Business Week*, 27/10/2003, Issue 3855.

[3] Maura Sheehy, *Manhatten, Inc.*

would have accommodated the hard, belligerent lyrics and accounts of tenement living, violence and drugs. Simmons always refused to censor his artists, withstanding charges of lewdness and infuriating the guardians of public morality. He would prefer to contend with the disfavour of his distributors than compromise the music. Hip hop fans were responding to the authenticity of the music: as Simmons told one interviewer, 'rap is an expression of the attitudes of the performers and their audience'.[4]

'If it's real, don't change it', was Simmons' mantra for Def Jam – and it's this attitude that propelled the label's success. Within three years Def Jam dominated the music charts with albums from LL Cool J, the Beastie Boys and Run DMC. The label rapidly grew into a multimillion dollar entertainment company, spanning film, television and clothing. This success is itself an important part of Def Jam's brand: as one of the world's largest black-owned businesses, Def Jam is an icon of black achievement. Russell Simmons, the so-called 'CEO of hip hop', has become famous as an impresario of black urban culture.

BRAND STRATEGY

From the outset, Def Jam has presented images that are true to the coarse urban environment from which rap arose. The label carefully avoided over-cultivating their artists with slick production, and consequently they stood apart from the ersatz glamour of black stars developed by major record labels. They were real, not untouchable. As Simmons put it, 'Our artists are people you can relate to. Michael Jackson is great for what he is, but you don't know anybody like that . . . It's important to look like your audience'.

Keeping close to the audience is at the heart of Def Jam's brand strategy. In the label's early days, radio stations and MTV would not play rap music, and Def Jam promoters such as Lyor Cohen were forced to use street-level marketing to generate word of mouth. Cohen, who is now president of the label, became a master of generating grass-roots buzz around new artists and new releases. Mainstream marketers in many

---

[4] Quoted by Nelson George in *Essence*, March 1988.

industries have since adopted Cohen's methods of seeding brands among the cooler influential kids and using them to drive momentum.

As well as the inner-city hip-hop fans, Def Jam's tough urban authenticity appealed to a broader audience: suburban white American kids. Hip hop's radically anti-authoritarian attitudes and sexually explicit lyrics were eagerly seized upon by the bored, rebellious, pubescent teenagers of middle America. Def Jam embraced this as an opportunity to turn rap into a mainstream genre, a mainstay of MTV and a business of major proportions. Def Jam continues to walk the fine line between 'selling-out' to mainstream commercial interests, and maintaining the genuine authenticity that has fuelled its success.

Cohen describes Def Jam as 'a lifestyle company that happens to sell music' – making clear the brand's emphasis on keeping close to its audience. In order to generate 'impressions' – and also to open up additional revenue streams – Def Jam has ventured into clothes, films, TV tie-ins and even videogames: Electronic Arts recently released a fight game – Def Jam Wrestling – featuring tracks from Def Jam artists and characters based upon the label's roster of rappers. This breadth of involvement in the lives of Def Jam's audience is essential to maintaining the brand's relevance and credibility.

THE ROLE OF THE BRAND

A brand represents a relationship with consumers – and in this respect Def Jam's brand is at the core of the label's success: keeping close to the audience continues to be the driving imperative for the company. 'Keepin' it real' – a phrase which is now a hollow cliché – was originally a guiding mantra for the Def Jam brand. And the audience loved it: the label thrived by turning unglossed artists from the inner cities into role models for young black kids, at a time when the cultural and political landscapes weren't providing many. As Def Jam artist Chuck D wrote: 'Most of my heroes don't appear on stamps.'

Russell Simmons recognized the potential for the Def Jam brand to play a role in inspiring urban youth, not just by providing positive role models, but also by organizing various activities. For example, the Urban Leaguer Def Jam Reader is a programme to encourage reading and develop computer skills in cities across the US, with the participation of Def Jam artists. As well as making a valuable social contribution, activities such as this reinforce the label's reputation for genuine grass-roots involvement.

Maintaining this level of involvement brings a crucial benefit: access to new talent. Def Jam has an enviable track record in launching new artists, and the brand plays a key role in two ways. Firstly, Def Jam has greater credibility within the hip hop community than most other labels, and artists have confidence that that they have a good chance of success. Secondly, Def Jam's reputation can bring greater press interest to new artist launches, and a more ready acceptance from music fans. In addition, the strength of Def Jam's brand may partly explain the loyalty that many artists feel towards the label.

Def Jam is positioned as a 'lifestyle brand' rather than purely a music brand, and this puts it in a strong position to face the dramatic changes forced upon the music industry by the developments in technology – particularly, file sharing on the Internet. Lyor Cohen, who is described by *Business Week* as 'a sort of post-Napster music exec', is bullish about the future. Def Jam's continued closeness to its audience, together with a talent for innovative promotional methods, has so far brought continued growth to the label. However, Cohen knows that Def Jam doesn't have the answers – the fans do:

> The answer isn't going to come from some finance type in a suit, so we better start listening to the kid with the braces, pockmarks, hair down to his shoulders – who wears the Slayer T-shirt. That's where the answer is.

FINANCIAL PERFORMANCE

As the global music industry contracts, Def Jam continues to show growth. In 2001, as worldwide sales shrank by 2.8%, Def Jam boosted sales by 36% to $960 million. In many ways the value of Def Jam's brand is self-evident: which other music label could release a successful videogame? It's hard to imagine Arista, EMI, Warner Bros or BMG venturing into brand extensions of this kind. A brand represents a close connection to consumers, and, in this sense, Def Jam's brand is crucial to its success.

Of course, Def Jam wasn't the only label to emerge from the early days of hip hop – a number of others were important players in the development of the genre, such as Sugar Hill, Enjoy, Tommy Boy and Profile. However, Def Jam has been by far the most successful at managing the transition from urban-cool to mainstream appeal. The core of this success has been Def Jam's confident refusal to compromise. As Russell Simmons wrote, 'I see hip hop as the new American mainstream. We don't change for you; you adapt to us.'

26

IBM

Culture isn't just one aspect of the game – it is the game.

Lou Gerstner

BACKGROUND

IBM is not just the world's largest information technology company – it's also the world's biggest business and technology service provider. Following the acquisition of PricewaterhouseCoopers (PwC) in 2002, IBM's revenue from services surpassed hardware revenue for the first time. IBM is also the largest IT financier in the world: IBM Global Financing has an asset base of around $35 billion. IBM is the third most valuable brand world wide, ranked after Coca-Cola and Microsoft in the 2002 Interbrand survey, published by *Business Week*.

HERITAGE

In 1911, the venerably named Computing–Tabulating–Recording company was formed through the merger of three companies – one of which dated back to 1890. IBM came into existence in 1924, when a new president, Thomas J. Watson, joined the company. Intent on overseas expansion, he renamed the company International Business Machines. Watson's IBM soon acquired some of the characteristics that remain to this day. An army of earnest, dark-suited salespeople espoused the business benefits of IBM machines, whilst industrious mathematicians and designers pushed forward the technologies. The company's slogan was, simply, 'THINK'.

Not many companies can claim to have shaped the modern world – in IBM's case, this would not be too much of an exaggeration. IBM innovations include the automatic calculator, the hard disk, the floppy disk, computer-programming languages, bar-code technology, the automatic teller machine (ATM) and, of course, the personal computer. No fewer than six IBM researchers have won Nobel prizes. IBM on-board computers facilitated the moon landings of the 1960s and 1970s, as well as the space shuttle. In 1997, an IBM computer called Deep Blue beat grand-master Kasparov in a chess tournament, fuelling speculation that the era of artificial intelligence is upon us. Indeed, computer freaks will tell you that the super-intelligent computer HAL in Stanley Kubrick's acclaimed film *2001: A Space Odyssey* was named in homage to IBM (according to film lore, the name H-A-L was derived by taking each letter of I-B-M and moving down one position in the alphabet).

By the mid-1960s, IBM's dominance over the industry was absolute – it *was* the industry. However, even as the company basked in its own success, an unprecedented crisis was approaching, one that would take IBM to the brink of being dismantled. At this point, IBM had never had to worry about the competition: there wasn't any – most major innovations in technology had originated from within IBM. Neither had the company needed to worry about really anticipating the requirements of customers: this was a company accustomed to creating new markets, to leading customers into *new* requirements. By the 1980s, IBM had become internally focused, complacent and dangerously uncompetitive.

What happened next is now the stuff of business-school legend – and an important part of IBM's brand heritage. As everyone knows, the information technology industry went into a period of extraordinary change: for the first time, IBM was plunged into a period of great uncertainty. The company's old, proud ways were no longer producing results: record losses began to pile up, and the company's stock fell through the floor. In 1992, the extent of the company's difficulties became headline news when an outburst by then-CEO John Akers leaked to the press: 'People don't realize how much trouble we're in.'

Figure 26.1   *This 1992* Wall Street Journal *story covers calls for the break-up of Big Blue*

Lou Gerstner took over as CEO in 1993, following mounting pressure to break the company into smaller units (Figure 26.1). By 1994, IBM was restored to profitability, and a sustained period of profitable growth ensued. This is widely regarded as a remarkable achievement. How did it happen?

ROLE OF THE BRAND

In the early 1990s, the so-called 'information revolution' was being driven by a number of agile, aggressive, smaller companies, led by crusading hyper-capitalists such as Larry Ellison, Steve Jobs and, of course, Bill Gates. Their work ethos was far removed from IBM's – they were young, hungry, enterprising and tireless. Rapid development and speed-to-market were top priorities, and 'just-good-enough' was the new mantra for the industry. This was all foreign to IBM, where releasing new products had become only slightly less protracted than the process of canonization. At the time, the joke at IBM was 'products aren't launched at IBM – they escape!'

Gerstner realized that IBM needed to respond to this, but in a way that was consistent with the brand's stature and heritage. Looking back at this period in his book *Who Said Elephants Can't Dance*, Gerstner writes:

> You could make fun of IBM all you liked. (Our competitors certainly did.) But for the issues that really mattered – when it was a question of national defense, or our childern's health, or serious scientific discovery – IBM was essential. Forgive my hyperbole, but in an industry increasingly run by mad scientists and pied pipers, we *needed* to succeed.

To respond to the challenges faced by IBM – while building on the strengths of the company – Gerstner had three broad actions: simplify, centralize and advertise.

- **Simplify**   The convoluted bureaucracies and Byzantine hierarchies within IBM were replaced by a lighter, more effective structure, and a new sense of urgency was instilled into the company – 'constructive impatience', as Gerstner called it.
- **Centralize**   The regional fiefdoms and product-focused power bases were replaced by global industry teams with clearly customer-focused agendas. Large global clients with complex requirements needed to talk to just one company, not a dozen: 'Going to market as *one IBM*' became a centrepiece of the recovery program.
- **Advertise**   IBM's advertising was particularly ineffective, despite a formidable advertising spend. This was consolidated from some 40 different agencies into one – Ogilvy & Mather, which subsequently launched the lauded *Solutions for a Small Planet* campaign.

A crucial starting point for change was IBM's brand, which would play a crucial role in driving through the company's turnaround, and consolidating the changes. By revitalizing the brand, Gerstner was able to establish and reinforced a new culture throughout IBM. The brand was key: structural or operational improvements would amount to nothing unless the company's culture embraced them. As Gerstner writes:

> The cultural transformation of the IBM's formerly successful and deeply entrenched culture – our single most important and critical task – will require constant reinforcement or the company could yet again succumb to the arrogance of success.

BRAND STRATEGY

In 1994, Gerstner famously told a press conference that the last thing IBM needed was a vision. As he later explained: 'Vision statements can create a sense of confidence – a sense of comfort – that is truly dangerous . . . in and of themselves they are useless in terms of pointing out how the institution is going to turn an aspirational goal into a reality.' Revitalizing IBM's brand was more fundamental than creating a vision. It was about establishing a set of truths about the company – and burnishing the company's bruised sense of identity. In practical terms, the launch of IBM's *Solutions for a Small Planet* campaign established the following facts about the company:

- IBM was a large, truly global company, and would not be broken into smaller companies. The campaign turned the company's size – once perceived as a potential weakness – into a source of brand strength.
- IBM was able to take bold decisions and act quickly – the scale and confidence of the campaign in itself re-established the scale and confidence of the company, in the eyes of all stakeholders.
- IBM became *humanized* – the machine-like Big Blue corporation now had a new, human face, as the innovative advertising showed old Parisians and Czech nuns talking in their native languages, with subtitles. The campaign was to show IBM as personal and accessible.

And perhaps most significantly:

- IBM was primarily known as a technology manufacturer – and now it was also a provider of business solutions. With the passing of time, this sounds like a generic strategy, but in 1994 it was a revolution for IBM: no longer did the company focus on the size of its mainframes or the speed of its servers, but on the business benefits that IBM technologies could bring to its customers. With hindsight, this seems like basic good practice in marketing, yet IBM was the first technology player to refocus its brand in this way: *Solutions for a Small Planet* claimed the industry high ground for IBM.

The emphasis on the brand was part of IBM's new focus on customers. IBM's new head of marketing. Abby Kohnstamm, recognized that customers do not base their decisions on a purely rational evaluation of products: 'All decision making, whether you're buying a jet airplane or a box of Jell-O, has both a rational and an emotional component to it: it's both a left- and a right-brain activity.[1]

FINANCIAL PERFORMANCE

IBM avoided being dismantled into smaller 'baby blues', staying instead as a world-class integrator – against the advice of industry analysts. The company's historic turnaround has resulted in consistent revenues and earnings per share (Figure 26.2).

---

[1] Abby Kohnstamm, quoted in 'IBM's Marketing Visionary', *Sales & Marketing Management*, Sept 2000, Vol. 152, Issue 9.

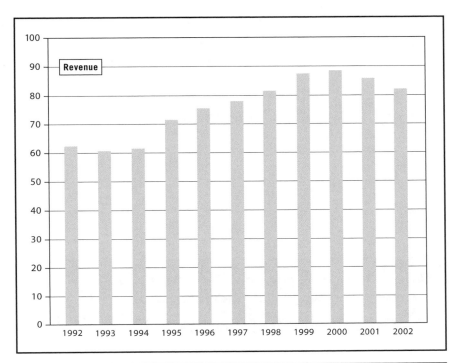

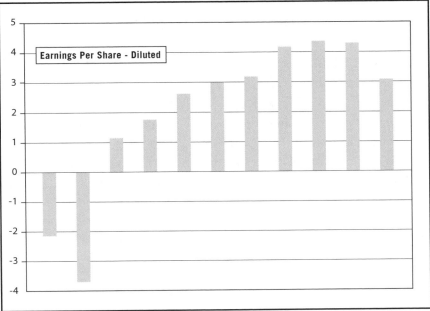

Figure 26.2   *Revenues ($ bn) and earnings per share ($) 1992–2002*

27

Dove

I believe a strong brand gives you options – and launching new products or services is probably the most valuable option of all.

Niall FitzGerald

BACKGROUND

Dove is a €2.5 billion brand – the world's number one cleansing brand. It encompasses a broad range of personal care products, including bar soap, shower cream, shampoo and deodorants. Dove is as global as any brand can claim to be: it sells in over 80 countries, and is the no. 1 or no. 2 brand in most of those countries. As recently as 1990, however, Dove was known mainly as a soap bar in the US. The growth of Dove has been extremely rapid, fuelled by a potent mixture of brand extension and global expansion. During the 1990s, sales growth averaged 25%. The brand continues to pursue aggressive growth: in 2002 alone, for example, Dove rolled out its new hair-care products into 31 new countries.

HERITAGE

The cornerstone of the Dove brand is the soap bar – which, strictly speaking, isn't soap at all: it's a synthetic cream bar developed by the US military, who needed a product that would lather in sea-water. When the product was launched to the US consumer market in 1956, a brand strategy needed to be developed: what exactly is being sold, and to whom? The brand position was designed by David Ogilvy, who joked, 'I could have positioned it as a tough cleaning product for the dirty hands of working men'. However, Ogilvy recognized that creaminess suggested luxury, and so the product was launched to women with the promise 'Dove creams your skin while you wash'. An early Dove print advertisement can be seen in Figure 27.1.

In an era when mass-market soap was seen as a relatively functional product, Dove's positioning was an immediate success, and the brand quickly became established in the bathrooms of America.

Figure 27.1   *An early Dove print advertisement*

ROLE OF THE BRAND

From the perspective of business growth, the Dove brand has played a dual role: to provide options for (a) extension into new country markets, and (b) extension into new product areas.

To provide options for extension into new country markets

Dove's impressive expansion into new markets is based upon a consistent, well-defined brand position – one that is based upon some underlying themes that are true of women world wide. Consumers associate Dove with qualities such as 'mild', 'gentle' and 'moisturizing'. Building on this, Dove has developed advertising that positions the brand as nurturing, as honest, for real women – a brand that delivers soft skin for natural beauty. This is at the heart of Dove's universal appeal; as Shelly Lazarus puts it,

> Cultural differences aside, people are more alike than not, and I don't know any woman who doesn't want naturally beautiful skin. Today, Dove is the same brand in every country, although each execution is unique to the country in which it runs.

Dove's brand position defines how these products are launched in new markets – in ways that make sense to the local cultural context. Take, for example, a launch campaign in Sweden, which encapsulated the brand's nurturing and restorative values in ways that would appeal to Swedish women. The campaign was based around the idea of a Dove Spa: women could visit the Spa at a natural hot springs resort, which was also featured in the advertising. Dove has successfully balanced a strong, clear brand position with sensitivity to local market nuances.

To provide options for extension into new product areas

As we've seen, Dove began as a soap bar, and now encompasses body washes, shower creams, deodorants, shampoos and conditioners. It has evolved from a brand closely associated with a specific product, into a brand with a broader appeal. Shelly Lazarus describes Dove as 'a brand with meaning that goes way beyond specific functionality – it can allow for additional Dove products'.

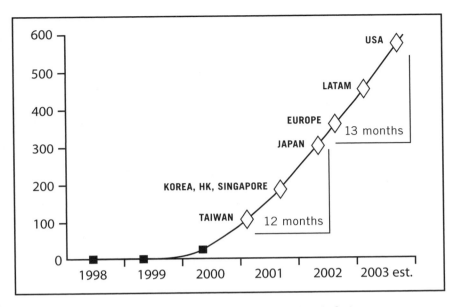

Figure 27.2 *Dove Hair Roll-Out (NPS €m)*

In other words, Dove has become a master-brand – a brand so strong and so well understood that it can sustain product extensions. The recent worldwide launch of hair care products is a case in point. When Dove Shampoo was launched in Japan – the world's second biggest hair care market – it rocketed to the number two position in just over a year. Successful launches followed across Asia, Europe and the US.

The existing strength of Dove's brand is the major factor behind successful extensions such as this. Having already established Dove's position as gentle and moisturizing, these properties were easily transferred to Dove's hair care range (Figure 27.2). As Dove's global brand director Silvia Lagnado puts it: 'It's a natural move, so consumers are not really surprised we're doing it.'[1]

FINANCIAL PERFORMANCE

Dove is owned by Unilever Plc, and is the largest brand in their Home and Personal Care division – which includes brands such as Lux, Sunsilk, Snuggle, Cif, Pond's and Axe/Lynx. These are some of Unilever's so-

---

[1] Silvia Lagnado, quoted in 'Natural move from skin to hair' case study on Unilever.com.

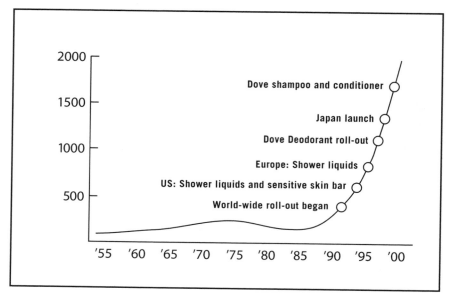

Figure 27.3   *Dove growth 1955–2000 (€m)*

called *power brands*: in 1999, the company announced that it would reduce the number of brands it operated from around 1600 to around 400. Of these, a small number of leading brands would drive growth and profitability for Unilever – and Dove is one of these.

In order to focus on these leading brands, Unilever has exited 110 businesses since making this announcement, accruing some €72 billion in sales proceeds. The criteria of which brands to dispose of included an assessment of the options for growth. As Niall FitzGerald commented, 'We agreed that decisions will be based, not only on the size of brands today, but also on their potential for profitable growth in the future.'[2]

Dove has an impressive track record of delivering profitable growth, as Figure 27.3 testifies. Leveraging the strength of the Dove brand, Unilever has built a substantial business, with annual sales in excess of €2.5 billion. Dove is an example of what can be achieved by creatively exploiting the options presented by a brand – options for extending into new country markets and new product areas.

---

[2] Niall FitzGerald, 'How and why Unilever favours power brands', *Advertising Age International*, October 1999.

28

BP

The brand creates a common future.
Michel van Eesbeeck, Head of Group Brand, BP Plc

BACKGROUND

BP is a large company with many activities. As a natural gas producer, it is the biggest in the US. As a fuel retailer, it has almost 30000 outlets world wide – giving it a greater retail presence than McDonald's. As an integrated oil company, it is the world's third largest, behind Exxon, Mobil and Royal Dutch/Shell. It is Europe's largest company, and the world's seventh largest. BP is a truly international company, having more than 100000 staff in over 100 countries. Every day, BP has more than 10 million interactions with customers world wide.

BP operates in a number of business areas, although its key strengths are in oil and gas exploration and production; the refining, marketing and supply of petroleum products; and the manufacturing and marketing of chemicals. It supports all its businesses with high-quality research and technology. For BP, the brand is about far more than communications: it's a powerful unifying force across the company's diverse activities.

HERITAGE

The early years of BP were fraught with risk and difficulty. In 1901, few people were prepared to endure the severe weather and difficult terrain of remote Persia (modern Iran) to search for oil. Few people, that is, apart from a wealthy Englishman – William Knox D'Arcy. After seven arduous years of exploration – and despite the absence of any infrastructure, the lack of labour and the difficulty of dealing with local tribes – D'Arcy struck oil.

Thus began The British Petroleum Company, as it was later to become known. One of the major influences in BP's history was its close ties with the British government. Winston Churchill selected the company to provide fuel for the Royal Navy, which was then the world's largest navy, with significant fuel requirements. The government took a majority share-holding in the company, which inevitably introduced a political dimension to the company's international operations. This continued until 1987, when the company was fully privatized by Margaret Thatcher.

By this time, BP and the other large oil companies were major economic entities in their own right. For such complex and powerful organizations, a clear and consistent brand became increasingly important. Corporate identity expert Wally Olins elaborates:

> [The oil companies] were, in their heyday, much more than just large international companies. They became almost separate geopolitical powers, negotiating on equal and sometimes superior terms with countries whose lands were fortunate enough to bear oil. Like nineteenth-century nation states, they needed to invent symbols in order to display their power in the outside world. Symbolism became important for diplomacy.[1]

This explains why major oil companies have always been highly committed to a single, powerful brand identity – across all business units and across all markets. Over many decades, BP, Elf, Exxon, Mobil and Shell have spent vast sums on extensive corporate identity programmes. They were – together with the large airlines – among the first companies to enforce consistent branding on such a scale.

---

[1] Wally Olins, *Corporate Identity*, Thames & Hudson, 1989.

Like its competitors, BP was seriously impacted by the two great price shocks of the 1970s (1973 and 1979/80). As a result of these upheavals BP decided to offset its dependency upon a single source of income by broadening into new areas of activity – from roadside services to food retailing, as well as investing in solar and renewable energy businesses. However, by the mid-1990s it became clear that BP's brand was hindering these efforts, for two main reasons.

- The strength of its brand as a petroleum company limited its credibility in some new business areas (though perhaps not as severely as the apocryphal tale of Shell's attempt to launch a mayonnaise brand).
- The perception of BP as a big, powerful oil company acquired negative overtones, as consumers began to become concerned about environmental issues, and suspicious of the power of large multinational corporations.

In addition, the late-1990s saw considerable acquisition activity, with nine major mergers within a five-year period. Given all of these factors, in 2000 BP launched a major re-branding initiative. As BP's head of brand, Michel van Eesbeeck, comments: 'The brand creates a common future, because we don't all share a common past.'

BRAND STRATEGY

For a large, diverse company like BP, an effective brand strategy is essential for maintaining cohesion and setting a clear direction. Indeed, as van Eesbeeck points out, 'for BP, brand strategy and corporate strategy are not separate things'. The re-branding of BP had two major components. Firstly, and most significantly, BP wanted to redefine its role in society: to be a constructive, positive force – a new company in an old industry. As the new brand position must express this, *Beyond Petroleum* was launched to provide a new sense of purpose for the organization. Secondly, there was the launch of a new corporate identity (see Figure 28.1), which clearly symbolized a dramatic change by breaking with the 70-year-old 'shield' motif. The visual change was significant, according to van Eesbeeck, because it 'gave everyone the same emotional challenge – both new employees and seasoned veterans'.

Figure 28.1 *BP's 'Helios' logo, designed by Landor Associates*

Beyond Petroleum was given substance by a number of commitments by BP: like any assertion from any brand, words must be met by deeds. These commitments are described along the following lines:

- Setting standards of behaviour in our relationships with everyone with whom we do business, based on the principle of respect and mutual advantage.
- Acknowledging the reality of climate change and the potential we hold to help to resolve an issue of which we are part.
- Setting targets, and progressively reducing the emissions from our products and our operations, and aiming to have a positive impact on the societies in which we operate.
- Being transparent, saying quite openly what we are doing, what decisions we are making and why.

BP is keen to demonstrate how seriously it takes the *Beyond Petroleum* position, publishing in-depth annual performance measures covering emissions, safety, spills and social impacts. Still, detractors such as Greenpeace remain vociferously critical of the company, accusing it of placing style over substance. BP chief executive Lord John Browne defends the company's re-branding:

> Some people think marketing is a word associated with manipulation and pretence – a concept that is part of a culture of mistrust and cynicism. On the contrary, marketing is about expressing a real purpose, and doing so in a way that huge numbers of people unfamiliar with the detail can understand easily.[2]

---

[2] John Browne, 'Beyond Petroleum: Marketing and the future success of BP', *Market Leader*, Issue 21, Summer 2003.

Lord Browne has very a broad definition of marketing: 'Every action and every activity is an act of marketing – an act of driving the creation of value through the development of relationships.' By providing a clear sense of purpose, the brand is able to galvanize all of the stakeholders – internal and external. Give people a sense of purpose, and they find it easier to align with the organization. In a sense, this is a new approach to brand strategy. As Mark Earls says, 'Increasingly, what's important is not a brand's *positioning*, but its *purpose*.'

FINANCIAL PERFORMANCE

According to Lord Browne, BP is a long-term business, and it's on this time-scale that the true value of BP's brand resides: 'BP's sustainability – its ability to continue to thrive and grow through times of great uncertainty, beyond anything we can ever predict – depends upon maintaining the confidence of a whole range of different groups.' Maintaining this level of confidence and trust – across very diverse groups of people – is the true role of BP's brand.

Of course, there are also more immediate benefits. Some uplift in sales, some increase in margins, and perhaps some reduced marketing and communications costs – but these aren't the real objectives for the company's brand strategy. It's the long view that most interests Lord Browne. Real, sustainable financial performance will be achieved when the company's values are aligned with people's behaviours – and the brand can help to bring this about: 'If people understand the intent, they are more likely to align.'

This is the real value of a brand; and this is why BP has such a high level of commitment to its own brand. As Mark Earls explains:

> It's not only customers who will rally around a powerful purpose idea. Suppliers, recruits, journalists, government ministers, shareholders, and even competitors will be influenced by it. That's why, if you get it right, the brand is so central to business.

29

The Economist

I wouldn't admit it but it's great for impressing people.
Focus Group Respondent

BACKGROUND

The Economist is a leading source of information and analysis on international business and world affairs – and it's not just a magazine: the brand also covers a range of publications, an extensive website, conferences, and the Economist Intelligence Unit – which provides business intelligence and industry forecasts. *The Economist* brand has been around since 1843 – it's an established brand which is highly respected by readers and non-readers alike.

HERITAGE

For a long period, *The Economist* was read by a small but powerful group of people: leading ministers, industrialists and financiers were among the few thousand subscribers in the late 1800s. Woodrow Wilson became the first presidential reader, as *The Economist* grew under the editorship of Walter Bagehot, who took over in 1861, declaring 'the object of *The Economist* is to throw white light on the subjects within its range'.

The Economist likes to count history-makers among its readers. Nelson Mandela famously read the magazine during his long years of imprisonment on Robben Island. A TV advertisement for *The Economist* tells the story of a fellow prisoner persuading the guards to allow prisoners to read the magazine: this was how they kept up with world news – until the authorities realised that the paper was about rather more than economics.

Politically, *The Economist* thinks of itself as occupying the 'extreme centre'. It certainly has supported a mixed bag of causes – from penal reform and decolonization in the early days, to gun control and gay marriage in more recent years. But is has also supported the Americans in Vietnam, and backed conservatives such as Reagan and Thatcher. In all things, *The Economist* considers itself the enemy of privilege, pomposity and predictability.

BRAND STRATEGY

The Economist was one of the first major media titles to seriously commit to investing in its brand – as opposed to advertising the content of the next issue. Until the mid-1980s, the standard approach to boosting sales for newspapers and magazines was to promote week-by-week content. Conventionally, media brands have taken a fast-paced, short-term approach to building sales, which has resulted in content-led communications. *The Economist* was one of the first to break this mould, recognizing the potential roles its brand could play: boosting long-term circulation, increasing advertising premiums and presenting options for extending the brand into new areas.

In order to build the brand, *The Economist* embarked on a much-loved and highly praised advertising campaign (see Figure 29.1). Instead of selling the content, the campaign sought to dramatize the emotional benefit of reading the magazine. People clearly felt a link between reading *The Economist* and success – this much was evident from qualitative research[1]:

---

[1] Quoted in *The Success of the Economist's Success Stratetgy* – APG Creative Planning Awards 1993, by Laura Marks.

Figure 29.1 *The evolution of a brand campaign consistent look-and-feel and a message that adapts to changes in the business environment*

> There's always something in there which you can use to drop into conversations which make you seem really clever. I wouldn't admit it but it's great for impressing people.

> A lot of influential people read *The Economist*. I suppose there must be something in it.

The Economist's brand strategy builds on these latent beliefs: successful people read *The Economist* – it gives you the edge. *The Economist* would be a polarizing brand – either you get it, or you don't. At its launch in 1988, the brand campaign had the following basis:

> If you were a reader, you were part of an exclusive club of successful people. The price of admission was the price of a magazine. The creative guidelines insisted that the tone of the advertising reflect

Table 29.1   *The Economist*: adapting to changing times

Era	Environment	Proposition
1980s	Conspicuous consumption, power-lunches, yuppies, Thatcherism/ Reaganomics	'Gives you the edge in business'
Early-1990s	Struggle against recession, 'downsizing', negative equity, success is keeping your job	'Don't get caught out'
Late-1990s	Clinton/Blair, more 'inclusive' rhetoric, upturn, work/life balance, personal development	'Surpass yourself'
Early-2000s	World events: 911, Afghanistan/ Iraq, SARS, economic uncertainty, a touch of global paranoia	'Stay one step ahead'

the personality of the successful club – clever, urbane – with an undercurrent of wit to move the brand away from its somewhat stuffy image.[2]

The Economist has managed to maintain unflinching consistency in the look of the campaign and in its tone – while at the same time adapting it to a changing business environment. Table 29.1 gives some idea of the shifts that have taken place since the brand strategy was put in place in the 1980s.

FINANCIAL PERFORMANCE

The Economist's brand plays a significant part in the business's value chain. Of course there are other determinants of success – such as distribution, price and content. However, a study into the effectiveness of the brand

---

[2] Annabelle Watson and Clare Phillips, '*The Economist*: the importance of selling a brand not next week's issue', IPA Silver Award, 2002.

campaign concluded that there had been no significant change in these factors.[3] Competitor activity may also impact performance: the report points out that marketing spending by *The Economist*'s competitors *doubled* during the campaign, making an even stronger case for the brand's contribution to the magazine's success.

> ### More Readers
> The brand has attracted more readers to *The Economist*. During the brand campaign, circulation in the UK has increased by 64% (from 86 000 in 1988 to 141 000 in 2001) – and in a market that has shrunk by 20% over a similar period.

> ### More *Loyal* Readers
> Increasing customer loyalty means an increasing number of sub-scribers. Over the course of the campaign, the subscriber base has increased by 95% in the UK. In fact, the majority of readers of *The Economist* are now subscribers, as opposed to one-off purchasers.

> ### More *Quality* Readers
> *The Economist* brand campaign sought to separate the wheat from the chaff – either you get it, or you don't. Consequently, the mag-azine now attracts more of the right kind of readers: the propor-tion of ABs reading the magazine since 1988 has increased by around 10%

---

[3] See footnote 2.

More Advertising Revenue

A greater number of readers with the right profile means that *The Economist* can charge a premium for advertising space. Comparing like-with-like advertising space and costs for 1988 and 2001, an estimated extra revenue £19.5 million was accrued in 2001 alone.

More Revenues Through Brand Extension

The growing profitability of the business – together with the increasing strength of the brand – presented options for accessing new revenue streams. To date, *The Economist* has invested in an extensive website, a shop, and various other publications and ventures.

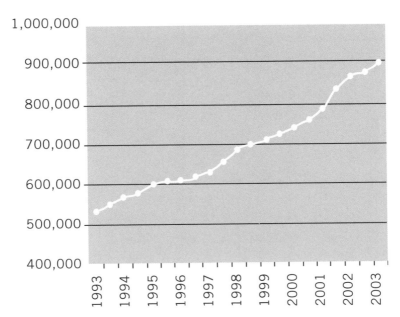

Figure 29.2 *Worldwide circulation of* The Economist (*source:* The Economist)

The strength of *The Economist*'s brand has clearly contributed to the growth of business. As well as fuelling growth in the UK, the iconic branding has become recognized internationally. *The Economist* has aggressively grown sales in overseas markets: Figure 29.2 shows the increase of worldwide circulation between 1993 and 2003. While the UK growth during that period stood at 46%, worldwide growth was an impressive 68%. The fastest growing region, supported by extensive brand advertising, was Asia – which grew at 85%.

PART V

Measurement and Valuation

> *Brands are fiendishly complicated, elusive, slippery, half-real/half virtual things. When CEO's try to think about brands their brains hurt.*
>
> **Jeremy Bullmore**

Brands are moving up the corporate agenda. Investment in brands is more than a year-on-year marketing expense — it is a strategic priority for any company. The brand can create value across a business, by enhancing business performance and providing a source of competitive advantage. The increasing importance of brands has been widely recognized: new accounting standards and tax legislation has been introduced to reflect the value that brands can add to the bottom line.

As brands have become an increasing focus for senior management, so a number of measurement-based models have been developed to enable a more commercial approach to brand strategy. In this part, we review these approaches.

Because they are intangible, any measurement of brands is ultimately built on sand, rather than rock. However, we believe a more commercial, numerate approach to understanding brands is still possible, and outline some possible approaches.

Increasingly, marketers will be required to present the 'business case' for marketing spending, and communications agencies will need to become fluent in the language of the bottom line. Accountancy firms are also becoming increasingly interested in a piece of the action:

There is a growing argument for a more numerate approach to brand strategy . . . The heightened interest in brand is driving us to merge accountancy and marketing techniques, in order to get a grip on this important area of investment.[1]

The suggestion that we might 'merge accountancy and marketing' may cause a cold chill to pass through many agencies. However, we believe that brand investment is a strategic priority for modern businesses, and there can be little doubt that brand strategies need to be presented in more 'hard-headed, commercial terms'.

---

[1] Laurie Young, global head of marketing, corporate finance and recovery at Pricewater-houseCoopers, in 'Brand calculations' published in *Brand Strategy*, June 2002.

30

Understanding Brand Strength

Which is the stronger brand: American Airlines, or British Airways? Many brands are clearly *strong* brands – Dove, Harrods, or PlayStation, for example – but *how* strong are they? How can we measure a brand's strength? What factors make one brand stronger than its competitors? Increasingly, these questions have become an important managerial issue, as brands take on a more central role within business organizations.

The measurement of a brand's strength has become known as *brand equity*. As a phrase, brand equity first started to appear regularly in the late 1980s, and the concept was developed significantly by David Aaker. He describes brand equity in the following terms:

> Brand equity is a set of assets (and liabilities) linked to a brand's name and symbol that adds to (or subtracts from) the value provided by a product or service to a firm and/or that firm's customers.[1]

In a sense, brand equity is a measure of the potential of a brand to add value to a business. Aaker identified four potential sources of value, and these are described in Figure 30.1. Effectively measuring brand equity brings a number of clear benefits:

- The process of measuring will uncover any areas of weakness, which can then be addressed.

---

[1] David Aaker, *Managing Brand Equity*, Free Press, 1991.

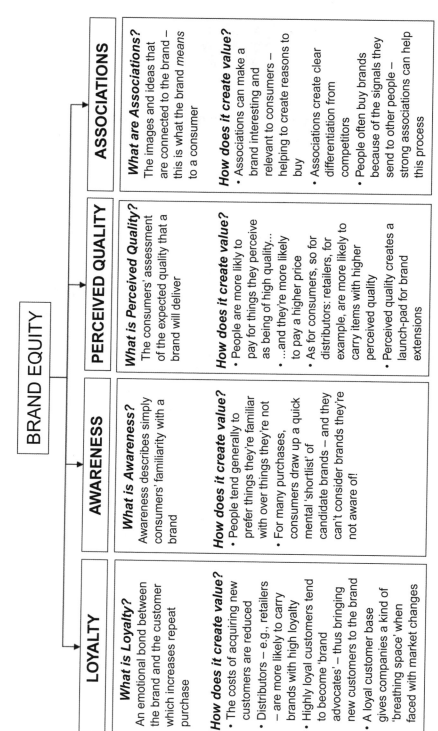

BRAND EQUITY

LOYALTY

What is Loyalty?
An emotional bond between the brand and the customer which increases repeat purchase

How does it create value?
- The costs of acquiring new customers are reduced
- Distributors – e.g., retailers – are more likely to carry brands with high loyalty
- Highly loyal customers tend to become 'brand advocates' – thus bringing new customers to the brand
- A loyal customer base gives companies a kind of 'breathing space' when faced with market changes

AWARENESS

What is Awareness?
Awareness describes simply consumers' familiarity with a brand

How does it create value?
- People tend generally to prefer things they're familiar with over things they're not
- For many purchases, consumers draw up a quick mental 'shortlist' of candidate brands – and they can't consider brands they're not aware of!

PERCEIVED QUALITY

What is Perceived Quality?
The consumers' assessment of the expected quality that a brand will deliver

How does it create value?
- People are more likely to pay for things they perceive as being of high quality... ...and they're more likely to pay a higher price
- As for consumers, so for distributors: retailers, for example, are more likely to carry items with higher perceived quality
- Perceived quality creates a launch-pad for brand extensions

ASSOCIATIONS

What are Associations?
The images and ideas that are connected to the brand – this is what the brand *means* to a consumer

How does it create value?
- Associations can make a brand interesting and relevant to consumers – helping to create reasons to buy
- Associations create clear differentiation from competitors
- People often buy brands because of the signals they send to other people – strong associations can help this process

Figure 30.1   Understanding brand equity – how brands create value for business

- The real sources of strength will be uncovered, which is useful for developing new products and services.
- A measure of brand equity can contribute to a financial valuation of the brand, so that the brand can be treated as an asset.

The interest in measuring brand equity was given particular emphasis by a spate of high-profile brand acquisitions throughout the 1990s. In 1988, for example, Nestlé paid £2.5 billion for Rowntree, although the company's net assets were valued at only £300 million: the real value to Nestlé lay in the strength of Rowntree's chocolate brands, such as Kit Kat. Developments such as this have driven investigation into brand equity and, consequently, a number of tools and methodologies have been developed to measure it. These are largely developed by marketing and communications agencies as proprietary tools with which to engage clients. We will examine the following:

1. Young & Rubicam's *Brand Asset Valuator*
2. Harris Interactive's *Equitrend*
3. WPP's *Brandz™*, developed by Millward Brown

PROPRIETARY METHODOLOGIES

#1: Brand Asset Valuator

The *Brand Asset Valuator* was one of the first models of brand equity developed off the back of Aaker's ground-breaking work. This was launched by the advertising agency Young & Rubicam in 1993, and now covers 19 800 brands in over 40 countries. The Brand Asset Valuator (BAV) outlines four building blocks of brand equity:

- Differentiation
- Relevance
- Esteem
- Knowledge.

Differentiation

This gives a measure of the distinction of a brand. According to the BAV, differentiation is the driver of choice and ultimately margin: it's the starting point for all strong brands. Good examples of brands with high levels of differentiation are Amazon and Starbucks, two relatively new brands. When Amazon first appeared there was literally nothing quite like it, and it presented a very different approach to buying books and CDs.

Brand differentiation (Figure 30.2) has been proved to impact margins. Using the BAV measure of differentiation the financial consultancy, Stern Stewart, recently compared companies that had grown their levels of differentiation with those who had seen their differentiation decline over a two-year period.[2] It found that those firms whose differentiation grew tended to have an operating margin of 10.5%, while those who saw differentiation decline had an average operating margin of 7%. It's also been observed that a fall in differentiation often precedes a long-term decline in business performance.

Figure 30.2 *Brands with growing differentiation have greater margins than brands with declining differentiation*

---

[2] Brand Asset Valuator, White Paper, Y & R Group.

Relevance

Differentiation alone is not enough: a brand must also be *relevant*. BAV™ also measures relevance – the extent to which consumers feel that a brand is relevant to them personally:

- it fulfils their specific need
- it 'fits in' with their lifestyle
- they feel 'this brand is for people like me'.

For example, many customers in the car market may acknowledge Porsche as highly different to lots of other cars. However, it is hardly likely to be relevant to the life of a mother who has five kids to ferry around. The BAV™ argues that brands with great relevance tend to have much higher market penetration rates and are likely to be around for longer periods.

Taken together, these two factors – relevance and differentiation – form a measure of brand strength. These will tend to be the first elements a brand develops when born, and the elements first to be lost when it wanes.

Esteem

Esteem measures the extent to which a brand is held in high regard and considered best in class – it's closely related to what Aaker would call perceived quality, and also includes an estimate of a brand's popularity. One of the strongest performing brands on this measure is Coca-Cola: it has very strong ratings for quality, and due to its global domination has strong scores for popularity. For managers developing new brands, esteem becomes the focus once differentiation and relevance have been established.

Knowledge

The final component of brand equity is *knowledge*. Under the BAV™ model, knowledge measures the extent to which consumers understand and have internalized what the brand stands for. Knowledge doesn't result from media weight alone: a brand must have a strong, clear idea which resonates with consumers. Knowledge, according to the BAV™ is 'the

end result of all of the marketing and communications efforts and experiences consumers have with a brand'.[3]

Taken together, esteem and knowledge are the building blocks of
brand stature. Brands which have good brand stature include Campbell's,
Mercedes and Ben & Jerry's. Brand stature tends to be a lagging indicator: a brand like Campbell's can have great stature but may lose brand
strength if threatened by new innovations (such as fresh soups in tetra
packs).

#2: Equitrend

Equitrend is a brand equity measure developed by research house Harris
Interactive, and is used predominantly in North America. It has three
key measures:

- Quality
- Salience
- Equity.

Quality is measured on a 10-point scale; 10 for outstanding, 5 for acceptable quality and 0 for unacceptable, poor quality. *Salience* measures the
percentage of respondents who have an opinion about the brand. *Equity*
is a measure of the overall goodwill associated with any brand. It is
calculated by multiplying quality with salience. Table 30.1 gives the
top scoring brands in the 2002 Equitrend survey.

The top Equitrend brands are not those commonly thought of as the
primary examples of strong branding. The predominance of functional
brands such as tools, speakers and foil is probably explained by the fact
that such brands very clearly deliver against expectations.

Equitrend provides an interesting way of comparing brands – although
it has several limitations.

---

[3] Source: BAV White Paper 2000.

Table 30.1   Harris Interactive® EquiTrend® Brand Study Fall 2002 Survey: Rankings among all brands Base: 30207 US respondents, approximately 2000 for each brand, conducted online.

Brand Rank Quality		Fall 2002			Spring 2002 Rank	Fall 2001
		Salience	Equity	Rank		
Waterford Crystal	1	8.29	61	50.7	11	2
Craftsman Tools	2	8.23	89	73.1	2	1
Crayola Crayons and Markers	3	8.20	92	75.8	6	7
Discovery Channel	4	8.20	92	75.7	1	4
Bose Stereo and Speaker Systems	5	8.18	69	56.8	4	6
M&M's Chocolate Candies	6	8.17	99	80.5	10	9
Mercedes-Benz Automobiles	7	8.13	68	55.3	12	19
Hershey's Kisses	8	8.12	98	79.8	3	8
TLC (The Learning Channel)	9	8.11	85	68.6	8	14
Reynolds Wrap Aluminum Foil	10	8.11	97	78.5	7	12

- It lacks the diagnostic to depth of the BAV™ or, as we will see, of *Brandz*™.
- It contains no real measure of brand loyalty, which ultimately is a significant driver of a brand's strength.
- It fails to capture dynamic changes in a brand's position as well as is done by the BAV™.

#3: *Brandz*™

WPP's *Brandz*™ is the most recent addition to brand equity diagnostic measures. The raw data for the *Brandz*™ study is collected annually by interviewing over 650000 consumers and professionals across 31 countries to compare 21000+ brands from a broad range of sectors. The results of the *Brandz*™ study can be seen in the 'Brand Dynamics Pyramid', which shows consumers' rational and emotional engagement with the brand over six levels.

The Brand Dynamics Pyramid

1. **Bonding**	They think the brand's advantages are unique 'It's my brand'
2. **Advantage**	They think it's better than most brands in category 'It's better than most others'
3. **Performance**	They think it's an acceptable quality 'It does what it's supposed to do'
4. **Relevance**	The brand meets their needs 'It's for people like me'
5. **Presence**	They're aware of the brand 'I've heard of it'
6. **No presence**	They haven't even heard of the brand '. . . ?'

Figure 30.3 shows an example of the pyramid, using an early study undertaken by the developers of Brandz™ at Millward Brown.[4] They took an average of all brands in the study, which shows that the typical brand has only 8% of customers at the highest level of engagement. The researchers also investigated the financial 'share of customer' for each level, and found that the value of customers increases as you move up the pyramid.

Brandz™ Voltage

Whereas a bonding score gives an indication of the strength of the brand, the voltage score is a one-number summary of the growth potential of a brand. *Brandz*™ Voltage takes into account how many people are very

---

[4] A. Farr. and P. Dyson. "Understanding, Measuring and Using Brand Equity" *ESOMAR* October 1996.

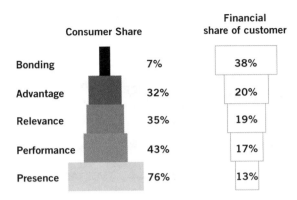

Figure 30.3 Brand Dynamics Pyramid and financial 'share of customer'

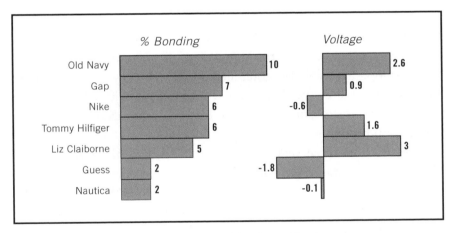

Figure 30.4 Brand bonding and voltage

loyal to the brand (the brand's *bonding* score) and claimed purchasing data for the category to produce a single brand voltage number. A voltage score may be either positive or negative:

- A brand with a ***positive voltage*** score has potential to gain share from its own marketing actions and resist the actions of competitors.
- A brand with a ***negative voltage*** score can still grow, but will have to work harder and over time it will be more vulnerable to the actions of other brands.

An example from the US apparel market is shown in Figure 30.4.

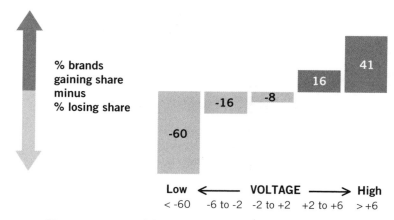

Figure 30.5 *Link between brand voltage and market share*

Although Nike and Tommy Hilfiger have the same percentage of consumers who are bonded with the brand, they have very different prospects.
Nike has a positive voltage score, meaning that it is more efficient than
Tommy Hilfiger at converting consumers up the pyramid. Old Navy is in
an even stronger position and is more likely to gain market share in the
future, as indicated by its voltage score.

After the first three years of collecting this data, the researchers at
Millward Brown wanted to validate the predictive power of the voltage
score – could it really forecast a change in market share? Mapping changes
in market share against Voltage™ proved a definite link between the two:
brands with strong Voltage™ were more likely to grow market share –
although brands with only moderate voltage weren't likely to increase
share by very much. The results of this study are illustrated in Figure 30.5.

So, Voltage™ has been found to have predicted change in market share
one to two years ahead – in fact, brands with a high voltage score
increased their market share in over 40% of cases. The advantage of the
Voltage™ score is that it gives brand teams and management a one
number summary of a brand's equity position. This allows them to focus
attention on how to develop the brand over time. We will also see later
how Voltage™ can explain more than just market share change.

31

Understanding Brand Value

APPROACHES

Approaches such as *Brandz*™ and BAV™ may have considerable diagnostic and predictive fire power, but they don't put an actual financial measure on the value of a brand. A number of techniques for valuing a brand emerged during the 1980s and 1990s, as the number of mergers and acquisitions involving brands increased. When attempting to place a financial measure on brands there are essentially five generic approaches one can take:

- Historic valuation
- Price premium valuation
- Royalty payments valuation
- Market valuation
- Future earnings valuation.

Historic valuation

Historic valuation involves looking at the investment that has been pumped into a brand over time. For example, Ford would look at the R&D they have invested, and the amount spent on marketing and advertising to support the brand. When taken over time this would amount to a significant brand value.

While this approach has the benefit of simplicity because it is easy to measure, it fails to capture the essential nature of brand value. Take, for example, the launch of New Coke in the US in the late 1980s. Coke spent years on R&D and opened the floodgates on advertising and promotional spend to support the launch of New Coke; however, the product died and Coke lost market share. If we had taken a historic valuation approach to this project we would have claimed that the Coke brand had increased in value – in reality, it had declined significantly. It is this focus on inputs – rather than outputs – that is the main weakness of this approach.

Price premium valuation

A price premium is the difference in price between a branded product and an unbranded equivalent product. This approach to valuation assumes that a price premium is the principal benefit conferred by a brand. The formula used is

$$\text{Volume} \times \text{Price premium} = \text{Brand value}$$

A good example would be Kellogg's. If Kellogg's sells 1 billion cartons of cereal in Europe and we find that on average it sells at a rough price premium of 30%. We can say that the brand in Europe is worth 300 million euros. There are three downsides to this approach.

Firstly, it takes no account of cost. Having a price premium is pointless if the associated costs of creating that premium are not met by the price charged. Couture fashion houses are a fantastic example of this. Stella McCartney, the famous British designer, announced in 2003 that her business had lost money. Now McCartney's clothes sell at a considerable premium, but she has obviously not be able to cover her cost.

Secondly, sometimes there is no generic to judge against in the market. For example, the 180-year-old American A1 Steak Sauce has no clear generic competitor and, therefore, it is very difficult for the brand managers of this business to compute its value using this method.

Thirdly, and closely related to the previous point, it is increasingly difficult to define what is generic. Returning to the Kellogg's example, supermarket own-labels are used as a rough guide to the generic price of the product. However, retailers themselves have exceptionally strong brands – for example, Tesco in the UK or Carrefour in France. If we use retailer brands as our base measure for the price of a generic, we may fundamentally underestimate the value of our own brand – essentially, the retailer branded products may themselves sell at a premium.

Royalty payments valuation

This commonly used method is based upon the assumptions that if a company didn't *own* its brand, but instead had to license it from a third party brand owner – then royalties on turnover would be payable to the third party, for the privilege of using the brand. Of course, a company that owns its own brand avoids these royalties – and this is taken to be the value of the brand to the company. The valuation is made by forecasting the likely value of earnings attributable to the brand, and then calculating the royalties that would be payable on this, if the brand were licensed. A limitation of this approach is that it does little to illuminate the source of value created by the brand, and is thus of little use in planning brand strategy.

Market valuation

Perhaps the best means to place a value on a product or service is to look at the price a buyer is prepared to pay – i.e. the market value. By clicking on E-Bay, we can get a good idea of the worldwide market clearing price for a 1968 Ford Mustang ($4650 today). Similarly, the price for which brands change hands in mergers or acquisitions provides a clear indication of their value. For example, in 1999 the German mobile telecoms giant Mannesmann bought the five-year-old brand, Orange, for £20 billion. The following year, Mannesmann was forced to sell the Orange brand, after being taken over by Vodafone. Orange was sold for £31 billion. In one year 'brand value' had increased by £11 billion.

This essentially displays the crucial difficulty with this approach. Market values are influenced by expectations of future earnings – and not all of these future earnings are related to the innate strength or weakness of the brand. When France Telecom valued Orange at £31 billion there was a strong expectation in financial markets that new technologies would yield significant growth and profit. The view today is less optimistic. In this case, the increase in value by £11 billion had perhaps more to do with market 'frothiness' than with Orange's brand value.

Future earnings valuation

This is perhaps the most well known of the financial measures of brand strength, and the most well used. The future earnings approach has been pioneered by two firms, Interbrand and Brand Finance. Here we will look at the approaches, and identify how they can be used. Firstly, it's important to understand the conceptual underpinnings of the approach.

The future earnings approach to valuing *brands* is based upon the financial market's approach to valuing *companies*. The value of a company's shares is known as its *market value*. The ratio between this market value and the net income is known as the *price earnings ratio* (P/E ratio).

$$\text{Price Earnings Ratio} \left(P/E \right) = \frac{\text{Market capitalization}}{\text{Net income}}$$

Similarly,

$$\text{Brand multiple} = \frac{\text{Brand equity}}{\text{Brand profitability}}$$

Therefore,

$$\text{Brand equity} = \text{Brand profitability} \times \text{Brand multiple}$$

Financial markets use the P/E ratio as an aid to valuing a company. For example, if an engineering firm in one year is generating net income of £100 million and the average P/E for a firm in its sector is 8, then the company would have a likely market value of £800 million – assuming that it will perform on the sector average.

The same approach can be applied to brands. In a sense, the value of a brand is really the value of the brand's future earnings. To estimate the value of the brand in the future we need to do two things: look at the company's sales, and decide how much of those sales are due its brand reputation.

PROPRIETARY METHODOLOGIES

Brand valuation #1: Interbrand

Probably the most well-known and comprehensive assessment of brand value is Interbrand's Global Brand Scoreboard, published annually by *Business Week*. This study ranks 100 global brands that have a value greater than $1 billion. In order to develop their valuation methodology, Interbrand went through the following five steps.

Step 1: Identify the factors that may impact a brand's value

Interbrand identified the following seven factors as the key to determining a brand's value: each of these has the potential to increase or decrease the value of the brand.

- *Market leadership*. Brands that lead their markets in share terms will tend to have more stable future earnings.
- *Stability*. Brands that have embedded themselves within the cultural fabric, like the BBC in the UK or Coke globally, will be in a secure and stable position, barring disaster.
- *Market*. Brands operating in markets that are growing or are well established are more valuable than those operating in declining or volatile markets.
- *Internationality*. Brands that have global reach tend to have greater stability in earnings, as they may be less affected by fluctuations in any one market.
- *Trend*. The underlying trend in brand earnings. As a rule, brands with a long-term trend of rising earnings are more likely to have those earnings continue to rise in the future.

Table 31.1   Interbrand Weightings

Interbrand factors	Weighting
Leadership	25
Stability	15
Market	10
Internationality	25
Trend	10
Support	10
Protection	5
Brand strength	*100*

- *Support.* Brands that have consistent marketing support and investment are more likely to have enhanced future growth prospects.
- *Protection.* Brands that have strong legal trademarking and protection are more likely to have a strong and stable future.

Step 2: Decide the relative importance of each factor

Of course, not all of these seven factors are of equal importance, so Interbrand has weighted them appropriately by giving each one a different maximum score – as shown in Table 31.1.

Step 3: Score the brands

The third step in valuing a brand is to score it. To show how this would work let's rank two brands. Brand A is a global colossus that exists in a stable market, and is either the number one or number two brand in virtually every market. Brand B, like the first, sits in a stable market but is much weaker and has little global spread. Table 31.2 shows how the ranking of these brands might look.

Step 4: Estimate the amount of earnings attributable to the brand

For some big companies, the brand isn't the major driver of their earnings. Microsoft, for example, may have a strong brand, but it's earnings are driven by structural and technical advantages. So, the next step in

Table 31.2 Scores for Brand A and Brand B

Interbrand factors	Brand A	Brand B
Leadership	20	7
Stability	12	7
Market	10	10
Internationality	22	12
Trend	7	5
Support	7	7
Protection	3	3
Brand strength	*81*	*51*

Table 31.3 Brand earnings for Brand A and Brand B

($ million)	Brand A	Brand B
Profit after tax (PAT)	200	150
Deduct overhead costs	(50)	(50)
Deduct profit not attributable to brand	(100)	(50)
Brand earnings	*50*	*50*

valuing a brand is to identify the earnings attributable to the brand. This is obviously made easier if there is a generic within the market that the brand can be compared against. Most often this is done via some form of estimation. Returning to our example of brands A and B, Interbrand would go through the analysis shown in Table 31.3, and we can now see the earnings directly attributable to the brands: in each case $50 million.

Step 5: Value the brands

The value of the brands are a function of both their brand strength score (Step 3) and their brand earnings estimate (Step 4). The simplest way to arrive at a valuation would simply be to multiply them. However, the effect of brand strength on business performance often isn't linear: up to a point, as a brand grows in strength, the positive impact on business increases exponentially. Thus Interbrand converts the brand strength

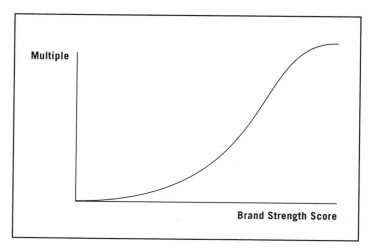

Figure 31.1   *Converting brand strength into a multiple*

Table 31.4   Brand values for Brand A and Brand B

	Brand A	Brand B
Brand earnings	50	50
Multiple	18	11
Brand earnings	*$900 million*	*$550 million*

score into a multiple by reading a value from an S-shaped graph, as shown in Figure 31.1.

In this instance our score of 78 for Brand A gives it a multiple of 18, while the weaker Brand B has a multiple of 11 (Table 31.4). What this means is that Brand A with sales of $50 million dollars and a brand multiple of 18 gives the brand a value of $900 million. While Brand B with its multiple of 11 and sales of $50 million is worth $550 million.

It is this approach which has allowed Interbrand to provide an annual survey of the worlds most valuable brands, shown in Table 31.5.

Brand valuation #2: Brand Finance

A second approach that is commonly used comes from the UK consultancy, Brand Finance. Instead of looking at an average of current brand

Table 31.5 Interbrand's global scorecard

2003 Brand rank	Brand name	2003 Brand value $m	2002 Brand value $m	Change in brand value (%)	Country
1	Coca-Cola	70.45	69.64	1	US
2	Microsoft	65.17	64.09	2	US
3	IBM	51.77	51.19	1	US
4	GE	42.34	41.31	2	US
5	Intel	31.11	30.86	1	US
6	Nokia	29.44	29.97	−2	Finland
7	Disney	28.04	29.26	−4	US
8	McDonald's	24.70	26.37	−6	US
9	Marlboro	22.18	24.15	−8	US
10	Mercedes	21.37	21.01	2	Germany
11	Toyota	20.78	19.45	7	Japan
12	Hewlett-Packard	19.86	16.78	18	US
13	Citibank	18.57	18.07	3	US
14	Ford	17.07	20.40	−16	US
15	American Express	16.83	16.29	3	US
16	Gillette	15.98	14.96	7	US
17	Cisco	15.79	16.22	−3	US
18	Honda	15.63	15.06	4	Japan
19	BMW	15.11	14.42	5	Germany
20	Sony	13.15	13.90	−5	Japan

earnings, this approach seeks to forecast future brand earnings. These are then adjusted – *discounted* – to reflect the 'time value of money' – i.e. the fact that a dollar today is worth more than a dollar a year from now. The valuation uses the following basic elements:

- *Financial forecast* – Cash flow from future sales over the next three to five years.
- *Branded Business Earnings* – The proportion of cash flow that can be attributed to the brand.

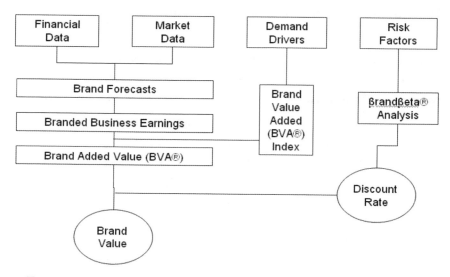

Figure 31.2   *Brand Finance Valuation Approach (© Brand Finance 2004)*

- *Demand drivers* – Factors that drive purchase behaviour in the category.
- *Brand Value Added* (BVA®) *Index* – Importance of brand in driving demand.
- *Risk factors* – A βrandβeta® analysis estimates potential risks to business.

These elements are used to calculate brand value. The process is illustrated in Figure 31.2.

In order to value a brand, we must go through the following steps – or 'workstreams'. We briefly examine each of these.

Workstream 1: Financial forecasts

The financial forecast is the basis from which the valuation is made – it's important to make sure that these are as accurate as possible. The valuation looks at all the factors that may affect the demand for the brand – ranging from economic conditions, through to new technologies, new legislation, and competitor activity, Once these factors have been considered, Branded Business Earnings forecast can be made.

Workstream 2: Calculate the Brand Value Added (BVA®)

This, according to Brand Finance, is the heart of any valuation. There are usually several key factors determining consumer demand, and the brand is only one of them. As we saw in the discussion of Interbrand's methodology, companies such as Microsoft rely more on structural and technological factors than upon the brand. The question is, then, how important is the brand in driving sales?

Possibly the most robust way of answering this question is to ask consumers. By drawing up a list of potential demand drivers, research can be undertaken to allow consumers to prioritize the factors that are important to them in making their purchase decision. Once the Demand Drivers are understood, a BVA® Index can be calculated and applied to the Branded Business Earnings from Workstream 1. This gives us an estimate of the BVA®.

Workstream 3: Assess the brand risk

As we mentioned above, the brand valuation is then adjusted to reflect both the 'time value of money' and also the amount of risk inherent in the client's business. This is done by calculating a 'discount rate'. Estimates of the time value of money can be calculated from economic data. The assessment of risk is based upon 10 criteria, as shown in Table 31.6 (10 is the best score, indicating minimum risk).

Once a risk score is assigned to the brand, this is converted in a *βrandβeta*® score, using the graph shown in Figure 31.3. A score of 100 would mean that the brand is exceptionally strong and hence the *βrandβeta*® would be 0, and if the brand was very weak the *βrandβeta*® would be 2. An average brand would have a *βrandβeta*® of 1. This is used to calculate the final discount rate to be used.

Workstream 4: Valuation and sensitivity analysis

The final valuation is done by applying the discount rate from Workstream 3 to the BVA® estimate from Workstream 2, as illustrated in Figure 31.2. The result gives the final brand value estimate. Brand Finance typically produce a 'sensitivity analysis' at this point, which indicates the effect on the valuation on altering certain key assumptions.

Table 31.6 Criteria for assessing risk (©Brand Finance 2004)

Attribute	Score
Time in market	0–10
Distribution	0–10
Market share	0–10
Market position	0–10
Sales growth	0–10
Price premium	0–10
Price elasticity	0–10
Marketing spend	0–10
Advertising awareness	0–10
Brand awareness	0–10
Total Score	0–100

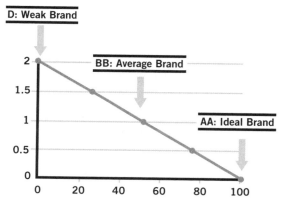

Figure 31.3   *βrandβeta® analysis (© Brand Finance 2004)*

Brand Valuation Example: Special Tours

Workstream 1: Financial Forecasting

In the Special Tours example (Table 31.7) we begin with a top line sales forecast. From this, we can calculate the branded business earnings – the amount of top line sales that result from branded products and services. These figures can then be forecasted five years

Table 31.7   Financial forecasts

Special tours ($million)	Base year	1	2	3	4	5
Top line sales	150	165	181.5	199.7	219.7	241.6
Branded business earnings	100	110	121	133.1	146.4	161.1
Operating margin	10	11	12.1	13.3	14.6	16.1
Tax (30%)	3	3.3	3.6	4	4.4	4.8
Net operating profit after tax	7	7.7	8.5	9.3	10.2	11.3
Net investment		4	4.4	4.8	5.3	5.9
Cash flow		3.7	4.1	4.5	4.9	5.4

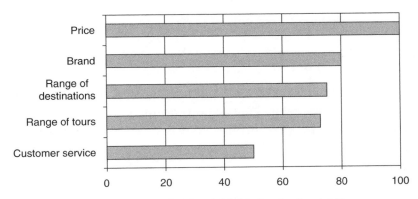

Figure 31.4   *Brand Value Added Index for Special Tours*

into the future. Finally, the cash flow forecasts can be generated, from which the brand will be valued.

Workstream 2: Brand Value Added

We then need to identify the main drivers of demand in the tourism category: they're likely to be price, brand, range of individual destinations, range of tour packages, and customer service standards. Consumer research might rank these drivers as shown in Figure 31.4.

Workstream 3: Assess Brand Risk

Having calculated the cash flows, we now need to calculate the discount rate – adjusted for risk by the *βrandβeta*®.

In order to estimate the discount rate, we use a concept from finance called the 'Capital Asset Pricing Model' (CAPM). This beautifully simple equation stipulates that, at the very least, an investor must get on any given project (a) what she could make without any risk (the risk-free rate), plus (b) compensation for taking the risk. This is measured by the beta of the specific company multiplied by the overall risk of the market.

$$\text{CAPM} = \text{Discount rate}$$
$$= \text{Risk-free rate} + \beta \, (\text{Return from market}$$
$$- \text{Return of risk free})$$

For the purposes of this example let's assume that the risk-free rate is 5.6%, and the market risk premium is 4.8%. She has also calculated the firm's beta, which is 1.5, since tour operators tend to be riskier businesses. Now she goes through the exercise to calculate her *βrandβeta*®. Let's say that the brand is strong and scores 75, this gives her a *βrandβeta*® of 0.5. Now she needs to plug in her numbers to get her discount rate.

$$\text{Discount rate} = 9.2\% = 5.6\% + 1.5 \times (4.8) \times 0.5$$

She then takes the discount rate and uses it to discount the cash flows as follows:

$$\frac{\text{CFP0}}{(1+\text{DR})0} + \frac{\text{CFP1}}{(1+\text{DR})1} + \cdots + \frac{\text{CFP}n}{(1+\text{DR})n}$$

where CFP is the cash flow period and DR is the discount rate.

This leads to cash flows with a present value of $16.7 million. However, the business is worth more than $16.7 million, because it is likely to be around longer than the five-year period outlined here. What most financiers do in this case is make an estimate of the

Table 31.8 Calculating the true value of the brand

($million)	Base year	1	2	3	4	5
Top line sales	150	165	181.5	199.7	219.6	241.6
Brand sales	100	110	121	133.1	146.4	161.1
Operating margin	10	11	12.1	13.3	14.6	16.1
Tax (30%)	3	3.3	3.6	4.0	4.4	4.8
NOPAT	7	7.7	8.5	9.3	10.2	11.3
Net Investment		4	4.4	4.8	5.3	5.9
Cash flow		3.7	4.1	4.5	4.9	5.4
Discount factor ($r = 9.2\%$)		0.92	0.84	0.77	0.70	0.64
Present value of cash flow		3.4	3.4	3.5	3.4	3.5
Cumulative present value	17.2					
Present value of residual	76.1					
Brand value	93.3					

business in perpetuity. This is sometimes referred to as the 'terminal value' or 'residual value'. In this case we have assumed that the residual value is the basic net operating profit after tax (NOPAT) of $7 million divided by the discount factor 9.2%, which gives a total value in perpetuity of $76 million.

In order to get the value of the brand we add the cumulative present value with the present value of the residual, giving a value of $93 million, as shown in Table 31.8.

This approach can be useful in kick-starting a dialogue between marketing and finance. However, the major downside with this approach is it can lead the unsophisticated into thinking this is a definitive answer. As with all models, this can be used to examine possible effects of various strategies, and to probe the assumptions behind these strategies.

CONCLUSIONS

The Brand Finance approach builds the notion of risk into the centre of the valuation – and this is what makes the method appealing. Intuitively, we feel that a weak brand provides greater stability to a business, and hence reduces the intrinsic risk of the business. A weak brand, however, doesn't protect the business and hence exposes the company to more risk.

An additional advantage of the Brand Finance approach is that it uses tools familiar to the finance community – and hence can help to build bridges between finance and marketing departments. This type of project is best done jointly between the two functions. The advantage for marketing as a discipline is clear: it helps to communicate the value of marketing by displaying a financial value to the assets that it creates.

A note of caution

- A brand can create value for a business in many ways other than generating sales – for example, attracting and retaining talented employees. However, the focus on Branded Business Earnings excludes these other sources for potential brand value.
- The $\beta rand\beta eta^{®}$ appears to produce a precise, objective measure – but it is based on a subjective analysis. These can lead us into a false sense of security: one should always aggressively question the underlying assumptions behind these seemingly, highly precise results.
- This information is clearly useful for representing brands in the balance sheet – but beyond that it's not clear how the information can be directly used to influence brand strategy.

32

Brand Measurement and Business Performance

MARKETING AND FINANCE: TWO CULTURES

British academic C.P. Snow wrote a devastating attack on the increasing separation between two academic cultures: the arts and the sciences. In particular, he castigated the arts establishment for showing little understanding and knowledge of fundamental basics in science.

> A good many times I have been present at gatherings of people who, by the standards of the traditional culture, are thought highly educated and who have with considerable gusto been expressing their incredulity at the illiteracy of scientists. Once or twice I have been provoked and have asked the company how many of them could describe the Second Law of Thermodynamics. The response was cold: it was also negative. Yet I was asking something which is about the scientific equivalent of: Have you read a work of Shakespeare's?[1]

Marketing departments frequently view the financial operation of a company with a similar lack of comprehension – or, indeed, interest. As a result, they are often viewed by many finance departments as 'unaccountable, untouchable, slippery and expensive'.[2] Ultimately, this level

---

[1] C.P. Snow, *The Two Cultures*. Cambridge University Press, 1993.
[2] M. McDonald, 'Key elements of world-class marketing', Speech at London Hilton, 5 March 2002.

of mistrust will lead to bad decision-making. C.P. Snow powerfully described the effects of a lack of a common language:

> It is leading us to interpret the past wrongly, to misjudge the present, and to deny our hopes of the future. It is making it difficult or impossible for us to take good action. . . . There is only one way out of all this: it is, of course, by rethinking our education.[3]

We would argue that brands are often interpreted wrongly, that brand investments are being misjudged, and that strong actions that strengthen business are being lost because of the lack of a common language. We seek to show how the marketer and the finance professional can develop a constructive and informed dialogue. Our attempt is based on two very simple cornerstones.

- Brands don't exist in boardrooms or factories. They exist in consumers' minds. As we saw in Brand Theme #2 (p. 5), *people* bring brands to life, not companies. Therefore any attempt to place value on a brand must have consumer measures of equity at its heart.
- Brands are no more and no less than a means to an end – ultimately, it is profitable growth that enriches stakeholders. Financial measures are therefore the final arbiter of a brand's success.

Therefore any approach to understanding the real business impact of brands must find a way to unite consumer measures with financial measures. We set out to do this, working with consultants A.T. Kearney, and using data from WPP's *Brandz*™ study. Specifically, we wanted to investigate the impact of brands in the following areas: market share, revenue, profitability and shareholder value.

THE BUSINESS IMPACT OF BRANDS

Earlier, we reviewed the forward-looking measure of brand strength, Voltage™. For this study, we used the Voltage™ scores for retailers in the UK and US (retailers were chosen since the brand and the financial entity

---

[3] See footnote 1.

are usually clearly identified – e.g. Home Depot brand is the same as Home Depot the financial entity).

#1: Strong brands grow market share

In the previous section we described how Voltage™ has been found to predict market share changes. Our investigation into market share for US and UK retailers further underlined this finding. As shown in Figure 32.1, high voltage scores for 1998 tended to indicate higher levels of market share in the following two years. This demonstrates again that strong brands really are more likely to grow market share.

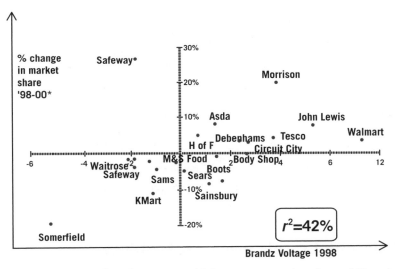

Figure 32.1 Strong brands are more likely to grow market share: US and UK retailers (Brandz™ Voltage 1998 vs Average Share Growth 1998–2000). T-Stat (statistically significant over 2.5) = 6.7

#2: Strong brands grow revenue

Figure 32.2 shows a strong relationship between Voltage™ and revenue growth. This is likely to happen for a variety of reasons. Firstly, a strong brand is likely to have a greater chance of earning a price premium, and hence increase revenues. Secondly, a strong brand creates greater demand and hence volume sales.

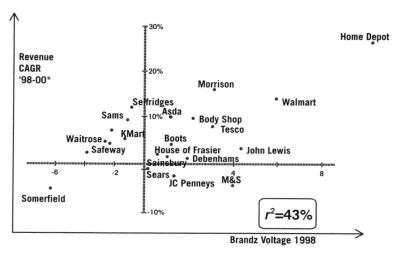

Figure 32.2 *Strong brands are more likely to grow top line revenues: US and UK retailers (Brandz™ Voltage 1998 vs Average Revenue Growth 1998–2000). T-Stat (statistically significant over 2.5) = 6.5*

#3: Strong brands grow profitability

Drilling down further to profitability, a strong link was found between Voltage™ and profit – suggesting that brand strength may explain much of the variation in gross profitability. We have previously explored a number of the reasons behind this. For example, a stronger brand is likely to command a significant price premium. Moreover, a strong brand may have high levels of behavioural and attitudinal loyalty, both among consumers and employees. As a result, the company may incur lower costs for consumer acquisition and employee recruitment.

Gross profitability tends to act as a good proxy (after accounting for depreciation and tax) for cash generation. With that in mind it was examined whether strong brands built shareholder value.

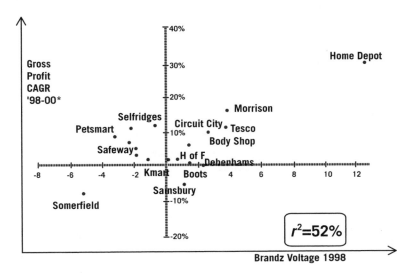

Figure 32.3 *Strong brands are more likely to grow profits: US and UK retailers (Brandz™ Voltage 1998 vs Average Profit Growth 1998–2000). T-Stat (statistically significant over 2.5) = 7.6*

#4: Strong brands build shareholder value

Shareholder value is measured by what is known as Total Shareholder Returns (TSR). TSR is determined by two things: changes in the share price, and the level of dividends paid out over time.

In the study, we found a significant relationship between the brand's strength (voltage) in 1998 and the TSR for the following two years. This is an exceptionally strong result which suggests that it is wrong to look at consumer and financial measures separately, since consumer measures such as Voltage™ can predict financial returns. The power of this approach is illustrated in the following case study.

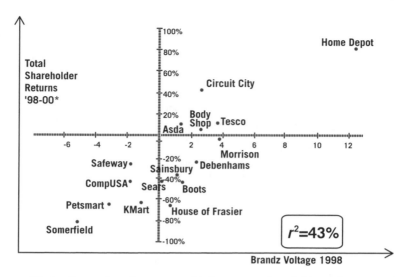

Figure 32.4 *Strong brands are more likely to grow shareholder value US and UK retailers (Brandz™ Voltage 1998 vs TRS 1998–2000). T-Stat (statistically significant over 2.5) = 14.8*

Case: A Tale of Two Retailers

Looking at the UK retail market in more detail, one can see the predictive qualities of this model. In 1998 Somerfield recorded one of the lowest scores seen on Brandz of –6.71. Somerfield was a weak number four/five brand with limited geographic presence. Its stores tended to have limited range due to their smaller sizes and the brand had suffered from weak and inconsistent promotion. However, at that time it was highly valued by financial analysts, and after the acquisition of Kwik Save stores, a discount retailer, this enhanced earnings per share for the retailer and the shares were marked up. Thus, in 1998 Somerfield outperformed the sector average.

Tesco also outperformed the sector average but initially failed to deliver the level of returns seen by Somerfield, despite having a high voltage score of 3.75. A number of factors contributed to the strength of Tesco's brand: they had exceptionally high levels of customer service and consistent levels of marketing support. Also,

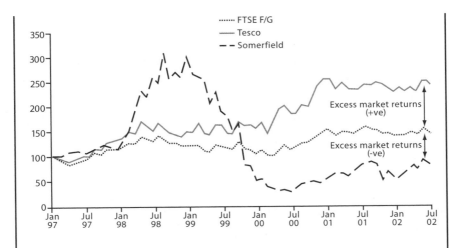

Figure 32.5 Share value changes for Tesco and Somerfield (1997–2002)

Tesco delivered value for customers by offering shopping in a range of formats – from hypermarket to small urban Metro stores.

In the long term, it was Tesco that created the most substantial levels of shareholder value, as it continued to outperform the FTSE Food and Grocery sector average. By contrast, Somerfield destroyed value, as it continued to lose customers and market share. The critical difference between the two is captured by the difference in their Voltage™ scores: ultimately no amount of financial engineering will protect a company from a weak brand.

#5: Strong brands reduce business risk

Our finding – that strong brands build shareholder value – is supported by several other studies. One such investigation offers a powerful explanation for why this should be the case: strong brands tend to build shareholder value because they *reduce business risk*.

The study[4] is based on a portfolio of the 'World's Most Valued Brands', as measured by Interbrand. One indication of the level of risk inherent

---

[4] T. Madden, F. Fehle and S. Fournier, *Brands Matter: An empirical investigation of brand building and shareholder returns.*

in a business is the *stock beta* – which measures the extent to which a particular stock is affected by movements in the market. The analysis found that the portfolio of strong brands had an average beta of 0.84 (i.e. if the market went down by 100%, the share would only go down by 84%). In contrast, a benchmark of other businesses had an average beta 1.07. (i.e. if the market went down by 100% less well-branded companies shares would go down by 107%).

This analysis can be taken one step further beyond proving a link between brand strength and business risk, to predicting business risk by looking at brand strength. We can do this by using consumer measures of brand equity – namely, our old friend 'Voltage™'. WPP's Millward Brown has shown that Voltage™ can predict business risk. Brands with a strong voltage have a much greater probability of gaining share (upside risk), while brands with a much lower voltage score had a much greater chance of losing share (downside risk).

Figures 32.6 and 32.7 present the findings from a study of over 300 brands. Combining these two diagrams together helps one to read off, for each level of voltage, the accompanying level of brand risk that can be expected, as shown in Figure 32.8. In this analysis the brands with top decile (top 10%) Voltage™ score a risk multiplier of 0.4, whereas a brand with bottom decile Voltage™ score has a risk multiplier of 1.5.

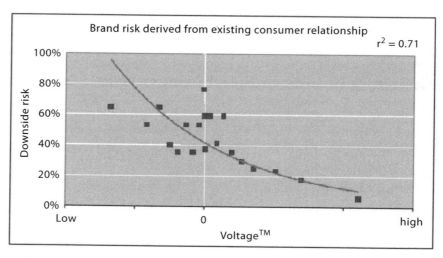

Figure 32.6 *Downside brand risk derived from existing consumer relationships*

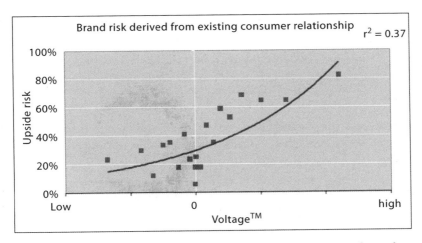

Figure 32.7   *Upside brand risk derived from existing consumer relationships*

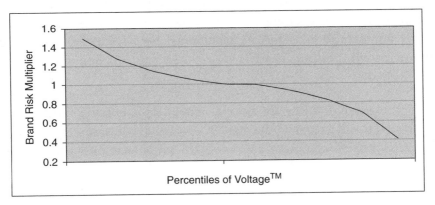

Figure 32.8   *Brand risk multiplier*

We believe this is a rich area for exploration. Protecting the company's bottom-line against risk is the responsibility of the CFO: the finding that strong brands have less systemic risk than other companies should promote their interest in brand strategy. Taking a risk-oriented view of brands may uncover new applications for brand strategy. Of course, this approach to brands also offers potentially valuable insights to investors.

#6: Strong brands create options

Sometimes the real value of a strong brand lies not in its present earning power – the cash flows it can generate for the business – but in the options it presents for the business to expand in the future. However, most approaches to valuing brands are based upon present earning power – measured by the discounted cash flow (DCF). Sometimes, this doesn't capture the real strategic value of a brand – its potential to grow into new business areas. As Unilever CEO, Niall FitzGerald, comments,

> I believe a strong brand gives you options – and launching new products or services is probably the most valuable option of all. It's a major dividend of investing in the brand.

This kind of thinking about brands is part of a broader movement in valuing assets, known as 'real options' theory. It holds that the real value of an asset – a brand, a factory, a client relationship – must account for the options it provides for growing business in the future. This seems intuitive, and already underpins much routine decision-making. For example, a study into business-to-business customer strategies found that many unprofitable accounts are maintained because of the options for future growth they present.[5] Here are some comments from respondents in the study:

- 'You might renew [the account] because it is high profile in the industry and it will get round the market' – in other words, this unprofitable account opens up options for new business contacts with other potential clients.
- 'We do it for the relationship. We do it because there might be other opportunities, like [new product]' – in other words, maintaining this unprofitable account keeps open the option to sell in new products or services to this client.
- 'If you just write it off, you have never got the opportunity to get anything back on it' – in other words, there is uncertainty about the future and keeping this unprofitable account reserves the option of benefiting from any potential upside.

These three examples demonstrate that the present profitability of an asset doesn't necessarily capture its full strategic value to the business.

---

[5] Keith Ward and Lynette Ryals, 'Latest thinking on attaching a financial value to marketing strategy: through brands to valuing relationships'.

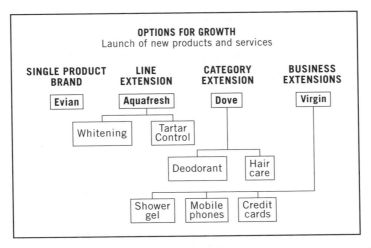

Figure 32.9 Options for growth through brand extension – some examples

The same applies to brands: in addition to the present earnings a brand may represent, its full value to the business includes the options it presents for expanding into new areas. As a result of this, many financial analysts in the late 1990s started to use 'real options' as a means of valuing businesses.

Strong brands create the real option of expansion of brand: they have a good reputation with customers, they have the trust of consumers, and they have the credibility to launch into new areas. Thus IBM was able to expand from hardware into services, and Dove could move from soap bars into hair care and deodorant.

There are a number of different levels of options for extending a brand – and these are outlined in Figure 32.9. A brand like Aquafresh, for example, may have the option to launch a *line extension* (such as mouthwash), a *category extension* (such as chewing gum) or perhaps even a *business extension* (such as dental insurance). The likely success of any of these ventures – and hence the strength of the option – will depend upon the strength of the Aquafresh brand.

An Options Example: Ace Computers

We explore the practical application of options thinking with an example. Take a brand called Ace Computers. This company could invest $100 million in the brand – for example, in marketing com-

YEAR 1   **YEAR 2**   **PAYOFF**

$135m ⟶ [$135m - $100 = $35]

$90m

$60m ⟶ [0]

Figure 32.10   *The option to expand into new markets – potential payoff*

munications. In the same year, this investment is likely to generate sales of $90 million. In other words, there is no payback: this particular business case is unlikely to make it past the finance director.

Net Present Value $= -\$100 + \$90$ million $= -\$10$ million

The picture changes if we take an options approach to the situation. Looking at the problem more deeply, we see that there is an additional potential payback (Figure 32.10). Apart from the additional $90 million sales uplift in the existing hardware business, investing in the brand could provide the credibility to move into the IT consultancy business. This would expose the business to sales of $135 million. In other words, the brand is giving the option to expand into new markets. Of course, if the company does not invest in this brand advertising, the option no longer exists.

However, with every option there is a level of uncertainty. In this case, there's an inherent risk that the new positioning could go down badly, and the campaign would backfire. Not only would Ace Computers fail to move into the IT consultancy sector, but it would also reduce sales in its core hardware business – in which case sales may slump to $60 million. Of course, if the company doesn't invest in the brand advertising, then this risk no longer exists.

So, if Ace Computers makes the brand investment, it acquires the potential to expand into new business areas: an upside of $35 million ($135 additional sales, less $100 advertising spend). However, the positioning isn't a sure bet because the business could be a dog. As a result, the team estimates that the company exposes itself to a new risk – a potential loss of $40 ($60 million sales, less $100 spend). So, making this investment may create a new option for the business – but given the potential upside and downside, what really is the value of this option?

This scenario lends itself beautifully to the 'binomial' method of option valuation. Simply, in order to determine the value of an option, we need to estimate the probability of the upside, and the probability of the downside. We also need to know the risk-free rate – the lowest level of possible investment risk, usually taken to be the interest on government bonds. Once we have these variables, the value of the option is found as follows:

$$\text{Option value} = \frac{(\text{Probability of upside} \times \text{Upside}) + (\text{Probability of downside} \times \text{Downside})}{1 + \text{Risk-free interest rate}}$$

So, how do we determine the probability of the upside, and of the downside? Since these are unknown, we have to find a way to *imply* them. In a risk-neutral world – and one where we are exploring two possible outcomes – we can assume that the probability of upside plus the probability of downside is equal to the risk-free rate. We can then imply the probabilities of the different outcomes. The probability of the upside can then be calculated as follows:

$$\text{Probability of upside} = \frac{\text{Risk-free rate} + \%\text{Downside}}{\%\text{Upside} - \%\text{Downside}}$$

In the case of Ace Computers, let's assume that the risk-free rate is 5%. The percentage downside is 33% (a $60m return on $90m) and the percentage upside is 50% (a $135m return on $90m). Thus we can calculate the probability of upside for Ace Computers.

$$\text{Probability of upside} = \frac{5\% - (-33\%)}{50\% - (-33\%)} = \frac{38\%}{83\%} = 46\%$$

Now we can calculate the option to expand Ace Computers into the high-growing IT consultancy market. In the case that our approach works (our upside) the project generates a benefit of $35 million ($135 million in sales – $100 million in marketing communications). In the downside our project is worth nothing ($60 million is worth less than our exercise price of $90 million) – remember options protect us from downside risk so unlike the project being worth a –$30 million it is simply worth 0. Hence the value of the option is:

$$\text{Option value} = \frac{(46\% \times \$35) + (54\% \times 0)}{1.05} = \$15.3 \text{ million}$$

Taking into account the first-year guaranteed sales of $90 million the project has a NPV of $5.3 million dollars when you include the option to expand into new markets. In other words, that brand value has increased by $5.3 million because the brand is now able to expand into new markets like IT consultancy.

How to apply to business

This is a very simple example of how to think strategically about the marketing actions one takes. As can be seen, probabilities are estimated and, as such, should be used as the starting point for discussion rather than a definitive answer. Discussing brand investment in terms of creating options can be useful for developing a shared agenda between marketing and finance.[6]

BRANDS AND MANAGEMENT REPORTING

Throughout this book, we've demonstrated that brands have a central role to play in creating value for modern businesses. In the preceding

---

[6] There is a wealth of good literature on using options in the 'real world'. Probably the best and most useful publication is 'Real Options: A Practioners Guide' by Tom Copeland. This shows how real options have been used in different contexts and gives the reader a variety of practical case studies.

chapters, we've demonstrated the tangible impact that a strong brand can have on key business metrics. As we said in Part I, brand strategy is business strategy. Given this, we would expect brand measures to feature prominently on top level management reports of business health.

However, the representation of brands in management reports is often woefully inadequate. The nearest measures are often things like 'customer satisfaction' and 'market share' – but these are not enough. Customer satisfaction scores, for example, very rarely predict strong performance. In contrast, Chapter 31 has demonstrated how certain measures of brand equity can give an indication of future business performance.

Developing management reports that neglect the brand are likely to provide an incomplete picture of the performance of the organization. Further, companies that do not properly reflect brand measures in their reports risk under-investing in their brands. While many businesses have implemented sophisticated reporting techniques, such as the balanced scorecard, these frequently omit brand measures. We would encourage all businesses to incorporate brand measures into their reporting structures.

BRAND AND BUSINESS SCENARIOS

We have seen how consumer measures of brand equity can be linked to underlying business performance – thus we can begin to develop a common language and understanding between finance and marketing departments. The following approach can help to foster this common language. Developing scenarios is a way of exploring the business impacts of various alternative investment routes.

The starting point for the workshop is to construct a very simple brand cash flow model. The building blocks of this are as follows:

Sales	Very simply looking at the sales forecast outputted from the brand plan – these can be 'best guess' figures or the result of more sophisticated modelling work.
Cost of sales	Next look at the cost of making those sales. That would include things like factory costs

	(for FMCG brands) or the cost of running a store (for retailers).
Operating profit	By subtracting these two items you are left with operating profit.
Marketing investment	All investments made to support the brand – from advertising to trade and sales promotion.
EBITDA	By subtracting the marketing costs and the brand's share of company overheads we arrive at EBITDA – 'earnings before interest, depreciation and amortization'.
NOPAT	After taking tax off we are left with NOPAT – 'net operating profit after tax'. This is a good proxy for cash flow.
Discount rate	The discount rate is used to adjust forecasted cash flows for changes in the value of money and for risks inherent in the business.
Residual value	Is the value of the businesses cash flow in perpetuity. In this case we have assumed that final year cash flows will continue in perpetuity.
Net present value	This is the present value of the business minus any investments made.

This information can easily be assembled into a simple spreadsheet model which can then be used as the basis for discussion between marketing and finance departments. Table 32.1 shows an example of the type of brand cash flow statement that can be put together – then we can begin constructing scenarios.

Table 32.1 Brand cash flow statement

Workshop Example	Base Year	1	2	3	4	5
Sales ($million)	25	25	25	25	25	25
Cost of Sales	18	18	18	18	18	18
Operating profit	7	7	7	7	7	7
Marketing investment	2	2	2	2	2	2
Overheads	0.5	0.5	0.5	0.5	0.5	0.5
EBITDA	4.5	4.5	4.5	4.5	4.5	4.5
Adjustments	0.1	0.1	0.1	0.1	0.1	0.1
NOPAT	4.4	4.4	4.4	4.4	4.4	4.4
Discount rate	10%	10%	10%	10%	10%	10%
Discount factor		0.91	0.82	0.74	0.67	0.61
Discounted cash flow		3.99	3.61	3.27	2.96	2.68
Residual Value						26
NPV ($million)						**42**

Scenario 1

What happens if we cut back the marketing spend? If sales are marketing elastic, say price elasticity is 1 (i.e. if price goes up by 1%, sales go down by 1%). In that case a cut of 2 million for one year will result in a sales decline of 2 million and we estimate it will take a time for sales to fully return. In that example our brand's value has decreased by $1 million (Table 32.2).

Table 32.2 Brand cash flow statement – Scenario 1

Workshop Example	Base Year	1	2	3	4	5
Sales ($million)	25	23	24	25	25	25
Cost of Sales	18	18	18	18	18	18
Operating profit	7	5	6	7	7	7
Marketing investment	2	0	2	2	2	2
Overheads	0.5	0.5	0.5	0.5	0.5	0.5
EBITDA	4.5	4.5	3.5	4.5	4.5	4.5
Adjustments	0.1	0.1	0.1	0.1	0.1	0.1
NOPAT	4.4	4.4	3.4	4.4	4.4	4.4
Discount rate	10%	10%	10%	10%	10%	10%
Discount factor		0.91	0.82	0.74	0.67	0.61
Discounted cash flow		3.99	2.79	3.27	2.96	2.68
Residual Value						26
NPV ($million)						**41**

Scenario 2

What happens if we cut marketing support in one year, but instead fund a new factory which can produce the product more efficiently (i.e. we cut the cost of sale). Table 32.3 shows that this creates nearly $15 million in value for our brand.

Table 32.3   Brand cash flow statement – Scenario 2

Workshop Example

	Base Year	1	2	3	4	5
Sales ($million)	25	23	24	25	25	25
Cost of Sales	18	18	18	17	16	16
Operating profit	**7**	**5**	**6**	**8**	**9**	**9**
Marketing investment	2	0	2	2	2	2
Overheads	0.5	0.5	0.5	0.5	0.5	0.5
EBITDA	**4.5**	**4.5**	**3.5**	**5.5**	**6.5**	**6.5**
Adjustments	0.1	0.1	0.1	0.1	0.1	0.1
NOPAT	**4.4**	**4.4**	**3.4**	**5.4**	**6.4**	**6.4**
Discount rate	10%	10%	10%	10%	10%	10%
Discount factor		0.91	0.82	0.74	0.67	0.61
Discounted cash flow		3.99	2.79	4.01	4.31	3.90
Residual Value						38
NPV ($million)						**57**

Scenario 3

The greatest sensitivity this model has is towards the discount rate – and risk, measured by the Beta, is one of the key determinants of the discount rate. In this example we've made the following assumptions:

Factor	Value
Risk-Free rate – UK 100-year Average	5.6%
Market premium	4.8%
Beta	1
Brand multiplier	1

Using our CAPM model (see p. 232) the discount rate calculates to 10.4%. However, say that by looking at our Voltage™ we discover that our brand is in the lowest decile, then our multiplier goes up to 1.5, giving us a discount rate of 13% (Table 32.4). In our example the greater brand risk wipes $11 million off the value of the business.

This for us remains the key take-out for readers. A brand's real value comes from its ability to reduce risk to the business.

Table 32.4   Brand cash flow statement – Scenario 3

	Base Year	1	2	3	4	5
Sales ($million)	25	25	25	25	25	25
Cost of Sales	18	18	18	18	18	18
Operating profit	**7**	**7**	**7**	**7**	**7**	**7**
Marketing investment	2	2	2	2	2	2
Overheads	0.5	0.5	0.5	0.5	0.5	0.5
EBITDA	**4.5**	**4.5**	**4.5**	**4.5**	**4.5**	**4.5**
Adjustments	0.1	0.1	0.1	0.1	0.1	0.1
NOPAT	**4.4**	**4.4**	**4.4**	**4.4**	**4.4**	**4.4**
Discount rate	13%	13%	13%	13%	13%	13%
Discount factor		0.89	0.78	0.69	0.61	0.54
Discounted cash flow		3.9	3.5	3.1	2.7	2.4
Residual Value						17
NPV ($million)						**32**

33

Building Strong Brands

Strong brands can clearly boost business performance – that much is clear from the preceding chapters. But what makes a strong brand? An Ogilvy study revealed that strong brands the world over display some very simple characteristics – an understanding of which can provide some powerful lessons. In particular, an in-depth analysis of more than 4400 brands[1] revealed four factors that influence brand strength.

- *Affinity*   'It's my kind of brand'
- *Challenge*   'A brand that is making waves; challenging existing orthodoxy'
- *Fame*   'The most famous brand in the category'
- *Price*   'A brand that offers very good value for money.'

These four factors were found to be consistent across strong and weak brands, across countries and regions, and across categories. Of these factors, *Affinity*, *Challenge* and *Fame* are the real drivers of brand strength – they explain much of the difference between strong and weak brands, as shown in Figure 33.1. *Price* is a minor factor, and does not build bonding with consumers. We examine the principle drivers below.

---

[1] Analysis by Jane Hodson and Simeon Duckworth at Ogilvy using WPP Brandz™ Data.

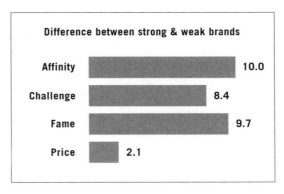

Figure 33.1 *Affinity, Challenge and Fame are the real drivers of brand strength*

THE DRIVERS OF BRAND STRENGTH

Affinity, Challenge and *Fame* are the principal drivers of brand strength. We look at each of these in turn. It's important to note that brands which sustain their advantage over the long term are almost always strong in *all* of these areas. They can be measured along the following lines:

- *Affinity.* Affinity means that people would respond positively to questions like 'I like this brand', 'it appeals more'.
- *Challenge.* For strong brands, people tend to respond warmly to questions like 'this brand is growing popular', 'this brand is setting trends', or other questions that suggest the brand in some way challenges the conventions of the category.
- *Fame.* Obviously, a brand is famous if lots of people have heard of it. Quantitative surveys such as *Brandz*™ can estimate the *Fame* of a brand in a number of ways: for example, by measuring how many people mention the brand when asked to name brands in that category.

Nokia is a good example of a brand that grew because consumers saw it as a challenger. Nokia stole leadership of the mobile phone industry from Motorola through classic challenger brand behaviour: it used its smallness as a strength, and introduced real innovations in communication (a prominent appearance in The Matrix) and product (a more intuitive menu). Nokia, it seemed, was the brand that set trends within its market.

Between 1998 and 2000, Nokia's brand strength (as measured by Bonding) increased by 14.5%, whereas Motorola struggled to stay still. Figure 33.2 shows that the principal driver of brand strength for Nokia was *Challenge*. Despite having greater *Fame* – as befits a market leader – Motorola was very weak in the other two drivers of brand strength, *Affinity* and *Challenge*.

By 2003 the story had changed, and a new challenger was on the scene: Samsung. For example, in the French market (see Figure 33.3) Samsung is showing a very strong performance on *Affinity*, *Fame* and, most impor-

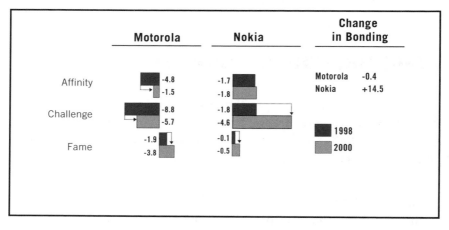

Figure 33.2 *Motorola's dominance was challenged by Nokia (Worldwide data 1998, 2000)*

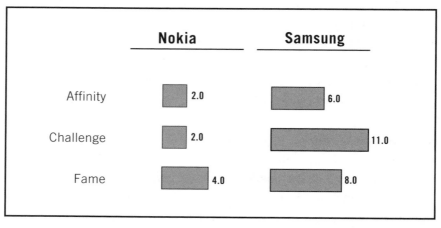

Figure 33.3 *Nokia's dominance is challenged by Samsung in France (France data 2003)*

tantly, *Challenge*. Nokia, although they have a good all-round position, are vulnerable according to this analysis.

Fame is an essential ingredient of a brand's strength – but, like the other drivers, *Fame* alone is not sufficient to maintain a brand. A good example is Volkswagen in Brazil – a brand which is part of the cultural fabric of the country. VW set up a series of huge plants in the early 1960s, and employs some 27000 Brazilians (even the current Brazilian president was a former VW employee). Volkswagen really was the people's car, offering relatively affordable transport for Brazil's emerging middle class in the tough years of the 1970s and 1980s.

The iconic status of this brand is reflected in its very large *Fame* score. However, it is weak on *Challenge* and *Affinity* – in other words, it's failing to set trends or appeal to consumers. New entrants such as Audi, on the other hand, have an inverse pattern: its high scores for *Challenge* and *Affinity* suggest that people see it as new, innovative and attractive. This is a significant threat for VW: although Audi is weak on *Fame*, this can be addressed by investment in brand communications.

An important lesson emerges from the cases of VW in Brazil and Nokia in France: strong brands must remain constantly vigilant in order to adapt to changing market conditions (this is explored in greater detail in Chapter 19: Maintain).

Part IV of this book looks in detail at some strong brands, and draws some lessons about building strong brands. For now, we look at a few examples of how *Affinity*, *Challenge* and *Fame* can come together to create real brand strength.

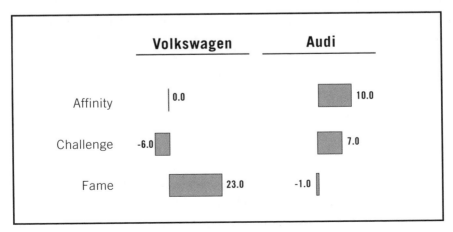

Figure 33.4 *Drivers of bonding for Volkswagen and Audi (Brazil data 2003)*

BUILDING STRONG BRANDS

#1: Mambo

Mambo is a 'surf lifestyle' company distributed throughout Asia and Europe, and originating from Australia. The brand is known for bringing together surfing, music and art – and so a definite attitude runs through all of their products, which include clothes, surfboards, eyewear, bags, books, posters and CDs. *Affinity*, *Challenge* and *Fame* have all played their part in building the strength of this brand.

Affinity

Mambo's customers genuinely feel that the company shares their interests – because it does. Dare Jennings, who founded the brand in 1984, wasn't simply interested in business: he loved surfing, loved art, and loved music. As he puts it, 'lucky for me, I knew what I was talking about – it wasn't a fashion that I was pursuing'. This genuine enthusiasm permeated everything the company did – and people responded to this, feeling a real sense of affinity with the company.

Challenge

Nothing the company does is conventional. Take, for example, the image shown in Figure 33.5, snapped on a recent visit to Manly Parade, a hot-potch of bars and surf shops in Sydney. Mambo's shop refuses to take part in the 'sale' convention, proudly proclaiming 'No Sale!', 'Why Pay Less?' and 'Free plastic bag with every purchase!' Mambo's has an irreverent attitude to the surf establishment, appealing to people who love the surf but don't want to become vacuous 'surf nazis'. Mambo has carefully walked the fine line between challenging the establishment and making the money: one of their 'Artistic Principles' declares 'Don't offend the rich until they've bought something'.

Fame

Mambo's has an instinct for courting controversy. For example, Mambo received plenty of publicity when hundreds of angry Christians picketed stores in protest at 'Aussie Jesus' designs. Mambo has frequently used its

Figure 33.5   *Mambo's proclamations in Manly Parade*

products as a platform for speaking out: for example, money was raised for Greenpeace when thousands bought a Mambo T-Shirt protesting against French testing of nuclear weapons in the Pacific – placing the brand at the centre of the mainstream news agenda. These activities have given Mambo a high profile. As with many strong brands, you either love it or hate it: when politicians complained about Mambo's 'disgraceful and offensive' images (farting dogs, vomiting dogs, used condoms, etc.) Mambo responded by publishing its *Company Standards for the Gratuitous Use of Toilet Humour*. The moral majority were not amused, but Mambo's fans loved it.

#2: Absolut

Not so long ago, Absolut was a Swedish vodka that even the Swedes didn't much like – but in 1979, some ambitious Swedish advertising types got together with the local distillers and hatched a plan to export the stuff. The story of Absolut illustrates how *Affinity*, *Challenge* and *Fame* can fuel the growth of a brand: in Absolut's case, from obscurity into the world's third largest liquor. For Absolut, the story starts with *Challenge*.

Challenge

Absolut was, by definition, a challenger. No one associated Sweden with authentic, quality vodka, and Absolut was an unknown entrant to a market where the established brands were Russian. In the 1980s, the conventional approach to marketing vodka was to establish the Russian pedigree of the distiller. Thus, advertising and labelling talked about heritage, the distilling process, the quality ingredients – all establishing the authenticity and quality of the product. Absolut took a very different approach. Instead of trying to persuade people of quality, Absolut *assumed* it. Instead of talking about purity, Absolut demonstrated it with clear bottle design and simple, clear advertising.

Affinity

Absolut wanted to position itself as a premium brand for sophisticated drinkers. When the advertising campaign was launched in New York in 1980, it was enthusiastically received by the media-savvy New York trendsetters. By commissioning well-known artists and designers to create the ads, Absolut have kept the campaign fresh – and because they really appreciate the advertising, Absolut's target audience feels an affinity with the brand. To underline this affinity, Absolut have consistently sponsored events associated with art, design and music – people almost expect to see them at private views and club openings.

Fame

Absolut has used advertising to create a buzz around the brand. For example, by commissioning leading artists to interpret the bottle, Absolut has generated plenty of editorial coverage in the design and lifestyle press. The wave of publicity that follows a new batch of advertising is far larger than the impact of the advertising alone. How many advertising campaigns have websites, TV coverage, books and exhibitions dedicated to them? Absolut's advertising – which has run for more than 20 years – has delivered more than fame: it's turned the brand into an icon.

Conclusion

If you believed everything you read about brands, you'd be forgiven for thinking that they are the answer to all of the world's woes. They're not, of course. Brands are not a cure for cancer, and they won't reverse global climate change. Neither, in case you were in any doubt, will brands cure baldness, shyness, ugliness or gross stupidity. And they're certainly not guaranteed to make you rich.

For many years, the hyperbole surrounding brands has alienated the more hard-headed and financially astute. For some, marketing always gave off the faint whiff of snake-oil, and the world of branding rarely held the attention of senior management. Now this is changing: there's a growing consensus that brand development is a priority for modern businesses. As Lord Browne of BP writes:

> Some people think marketing is a word associated with manipulation and pretence – a concept that is part of a culture of mistrust and cynicism. On the contrary, marketing is about expressing a real purpose, and doing so in a way that huge numbers of people unfamiliar with the detail can understand easily.[1]

Companies of all sizes, and across all kinds of markets, are bringing brand strategy to the heart of business strategy. By 'expressing a real purpose', a

---

[1] J Browne (Summer 2003) *Beyond Petroleum: Marketing and the future success of* BP Market Leader Issue 21.

brand can help to align the many stakeholders in an organization. By providing a kind of in-built market orientation across the business, a brand can answer the main strategic questions facing any business: who are our customers? What products and services will we offer?

In the preceding pages, we've seen countless examples of this in action – in companies as diverse as Rollerblade, BP, Mambo and IBM. We've seen the powerful role brands can play in enhancing business value: growing market share and profitability, reducing business risk, creating new business options, and delivering real value for shareholders. Properly understood, brands are an essential management tool.

However, during the course of writing this book, it became clear that many of the exponents of brands have a semi-religious faith in the power of branding. Brands are treated with an almost fetishistic obsession by legions of gurus, consultants and guardians. Sometimes it can seem as if brands are an end in themselves, instead of a tool to serve management objectives.

Brands are not, of course, an end in themselves. Brand strength is not an objective, but a strategy for attaining superior business performance. A brand can create a powerful sense of purpose – rallying not only customers, but also employees, suppliers, and shareholders. When all of these stakeholders are aligned, that's when the value-making really begins – and this is the real business of brands.

UNIVERSITY OF CHESTER, WARRINGTON CAMPUS

Index